Ablaze With His Glory!

Ablaze With His Glory!

Del Fehsenfeld Jr.

THOMAS NELSON PUBLISHERS
Nashville

Published in Nashville, Tennessee, by Thomas Nelson, Inc.,
Publishers, and distributed in Canada by Word Communications, Ltd.,
Richmond, British Columbia, and in the United Kingdom by Word
(UK), Ltd., Milton Keynes, England.

All scripture references are from the *King James Version* of the
Bible, unless noted otherwise.

Library of Congress Cataloging-in-Publication Data

Fehsenfeld, Del, d. 1989.
   Ablaze with His glory / by Del Fehsenfeld
      p. cm.
   ISBN 0-8407-6773-0 (pbk.)
    1. Church renewal—United States. 2. Revivals—United States. 3.
United States—Moral conditions. 4. Glory of God. I. Title.
BV600.2.F44 1993
269'.24—dc20   93-13172
                                                CIP

Printed in the United States of America
1 2 3 4 5 6 — 98 97 96 95 94 93

Contents

Part Four: Bring Back the Glory

Acknowledgments 171

About Life Action Ministries 173

End Notes 175

Dedication

Those who knew Del best believe that, had he lived to see this book published, he would have wanted to dedicate it to his father, Del Fehsenfeld Sr., under whose nurture he learned his earliest and greatest lessons about the heart and ways of God, and in whom he first witnessed a passionate longing for revival in the church.

Foreword

The message of Del Fehsenfeld Jr. is perhaps the most desperately needed message in our churches today.

In recent decades, it has become obvious that all our attempts to produce remedies for the ills of our society are utterly inadequate, apart from a fresh, supernatural invasion of God's Spirit into the life of His church.

The solutions to the sickness of our culture are never going to be found in the White House—they will only be found in the house of God! With Del, I believe that our only real hope is for God to revive His people.

Unfortunately, we as professing Christians have carried on our love affair with the world for so long, that few are able to perceive, much less grieve over, the extent to which the church has become "seasoned" by the philosophies and values of our godless world system. As a result, we have forfeited the ability to influence our world in any meaningful or effective way. The reproach is no longer in the message of Christ and His cross, but in the lives and institutions that proclaim that message.

Ablaze With His Glory pulsates with a heartcry that some may find difficult to receive. But it is a heartcry that must be both heard and heeded, if we are to see God send a spiritual awakening in our day.

This message comes from the pen of one of God's choice servants who faithfully proclaimed the message of revival to the church, until his death in 1989. Del Fehsenfeld Jr. had the heart of a "prophet," to sound an alarm and call the church back to repentance, holiness, and a rekindled "first love" for Christ.

The insights contained in this volume were birthed out of extensive, firsthand experience in the local church. Along with his family, Del spent two decades traveling the length and breadth of this continent, pleading with God's people to return to Him with all their hearts. He preached revival crusades lasting up to six weeks in hundreds of churches throughout North America. He was mightily used of God to impact thousands of lives for eternity.

In recent months, God has been doing a fresh work in my own heart, deepening my understanding of His ways, and giving me a new vision and burden for genuine revival. I believe now, more than ever, that this message must be proclaimed with intensity, urgency, and fervency.

As you read this book, my prayer is that God will ignite in your heart and in your church a spark that will become a flame of righteousness spreading across our land. May God soon grant our hearts' desire to see our lives, our churches, our nation, and ultimately, our world, ablaze with His glory!

Dr. Charles F. Stanley
Pastor, First Baptist Church, Atlanta

Introduction

Del Fehsenfeld Jr. was a man of one consuming passion—the glory of God. Nothing so thrilled him as the prospect of God's glory being manifested to our world through the lives of His people. And nothing so grieved him as the thought that we might in some way hinder the free flow of God's Spirit in our midst.

The thrust of Del's message was not so much against the evils of a lost world, as to the heart of the church, which he saw to be desperately in need of genuine, heaven-sent revival.

His preaching went against the tide of today's man-centered, narcissistic religion which is obsessed with feeling good. He believed that people would never truly be free until they came face to face with a holy God and were broken and repentant over their sin. He was always pointing people to the cross and to the resurrected Christ whose life could become operational in them through faith.

Del was a "family physician" for the church. He had a keen sense of the patient's pulse. Though many of his colleagues pronounced the body to be in tiptop shape, Del looked beyond the external evidence of soundness, to the soul of the church and knew that there was cause for grave concern.

In March of 1989, at the age of 42, Del was diagnosed with a malignant brain tumor which took his life seven months later. Rather than retreating from public ministry during the final months of his life, Del continued to preach until he was no longer physically able to do so. Though his body was weak, his ministry during that time was marked by an unusual sense of fervency, urgency, and intense burden for our nation and for the church.

He felt that the cancer in his own body was a picture of the sin and carnality that were destroying the body of Christ from the inside out. As in his own case, he knew that there was no human hope for the plight of the church, apart from miraculous, divine intervention.

Del dearly loved the church of Christ, shed many tears over it, and gave himself unstintingly to its care. He never gave up hope that God would indeed come and revive and restore it if we would simply humble ourselves, acknowledge our need, and meet His conditions. He never wavered in his conviction that God was going to purify and revive His bride before coming to take her to heaven. Like so many who preceded him, he "died in faith, not having received the promises, but having seen them afar off, and [was] persuaded of them . . ." (Heb. 11:13).

A day or so before he slipped into unconsciousness, when it had become very difficult for him to speak, Del broke a long period of what was thought to be sleep, with the following prayer:

> *"Lord, please bring back Your glory to Your church. Send the fire. Turn the hearts of Your people. May they know that You alone are God."*

This book is the legacy of a servant of God whose love for Christ and for His church was extraordinary and passionate. We are believing God to raise up in Del's place a host of surrendered men and women who will pick up the torch that Del carried so faithfully, and who will not let go of God until our churches and our land are once again ablaze with His glory.

—Life Action Ministries

Sound the Alarm

Part One

Chapter 1

The Darkness Is Coming

The warm California sunshine sparkled off the golden paint on the pastor's Cadillac as we drove off the church parking lot on our way to lunch. The beautiful homes of the affluent suburban neighborhood flashed past as we rolled along the palm-lined boulevard toward the restaurant.

"I don't know what's wrong with these people," the pastor lamented to me and an associate. "They are so materialistic and self-centered that I don't think they want revival."

I couldn't help wondering what connection there might be between the attitudes of the people and those of leadership as I settled into the cushy leather seat of the Sedan de Ville.

"How long have you been at this church?" I asked.

"Nearly ten years," he replied. "And nothing has really changed. If anything, things are worse!" he admitted.

"What about you?" I asked sincerely. "Do you have a desire for revival in your own heart?"

"To be honest," the pastor admitted, "I guess I've been too busy for revival. In fact, the whole church is too busy for revival!"

There had been a time when this church had been a real lighthouse for the gospel in Southern California, but as the crusade muddled on, it became increasingly obvious that the light was quickly burning out. The people seemed dull and preoccupied. In fact, the pastor seemed dull and preoccupied.

As we left the car with the valet attendant, I realized that this dear pastor was turning out just like his people—or they were turning out just like him!

He was a kind and gracious man. He was certainly generous enough. The meals were almost lavish, and he seemed to spare no expense trying to make us all happy. But the absence of the presence of God in the services was conspicuous. The people had no real heart for God or spiritual things. Some of them actually dabbled in other cults while professing to be born-again Christians. Their marriages were falling apart, and their homes were battle zones.

Talking to pastors about their problems has never been easy for me, so I was reluctant to comment on the situation at the church, but finally I felt compelled to do so.

"Pastor," I suggested cautiously, "it seems to me that you are at a serious crossroads. If the church does not experience genuine revival, I doubt that it can survive."

I wondered how he would take such a blunt observation, no matter how cautiously it was offered. To my surprise he said, "You're right! If we don't have revival, I am going to quit and the people will probably do the same." He went on to admit the church had been in spiritual decline for some time and questioned whether it was worth going ahead.

"What should we do?" I asked.

"That's why I brought you here," he announced.

"But I can't manufacture revival!" I protested. "If God doesn't send it, we won't have revival."

As we discussed the whole issue of true revival and the need for repentance on the part of God's people, he became more distant. "I'm not really into that kind of preaching," he acknowledged. "It seems to turn people off."

"How could they get any more turned off than they already are?" I asked. "The crowds are dwindling away to nothing, and nobody even seems to care. It's not just the crusade; it's that way every Sunday, isn't it?" I asked.

"It goes back to everybody being too busy," he suggested again.

"Then if they are too busy for God, they really are too busy!" I replied. "Something needs to change or God Himself may as well depart!"

The crusade was an utter failure. We encountered more opposition than in almost any meeting I had ever conducted. Even the associate pastor openly fought everything we tried to do, going so far as to post flyers denouncing revival. My heart was heavy as person after person admitted something was wrong, but nobody wanted to pay the price to correct it.

Within a month after the crusade closed, the pastor resigned. The people, in sheer frustration, voted to sell the building, liquidate the debts, and dissolve the church. For all practical purposes, the light of the gospel and the glorious presence of God were extinguished in that church because the pastor and people were too busy playing religion to get serious with God. In reality, the glory had departed long before we arrived. All we were able to do was examine the empty shell of what once had housed the presence of God. Had we been able to look upon that situation from heaven's vantage point, I wonder if we would have seen *Ichabod* ("the glory has departed") written somewhere upon the walls.

TIME TO WAKE UP

Even the most optimistic observer must admit that the escalation of social and moral ills in our society is alarming; pornography, adultery, divorce, abortion, alcoholism, and homosexuality have all become accepted elements of our social landscape.

Ours is a shattered society, strewn with the wreckage of broken hearts, lives, and relationships. Our political, civic, and religious leaders have exhausted their resources seeking human solutions to the great social evils of our time. Even our more successful remedies seem to be no more than bandages on hemorrhaging wounds.

These problems of our society are symptomatic of moral and spiritual decay so pervasive that it threatens our very existence. We can no longer afford the luxury of living for today, blindly disregarding the consequences of what we will certainly face tomorrow. Spiritual darkness is encroaching upon our land, threatening to plunge us into a new Dark Age.

THE ABSENCE OF TRUTH

The absence of the Word of God in our national life is undoubtedly one of the greatest factors in the deterioration of our society. In Hebrew, Proverbs 29:18 literally says, "Where there is no vision [revelation of God's Word], the people perish [or throw off all restraint]." That is exactly what is happening today. A lack of biblical truth in our national life has led to a drive to throw off all moral restraint.

The most significant social change of the past few decades has been the shift away from the absolutes of the Word of God. Without the Bible as the standard of God's truth and righteousness, man has no moral compass. He is left to do as he chooses. He has no accountability to God; therefore, man becomes a law unto himself.

What is the result? An epidemic of evil has swept over our land. Marriages are breaking up; parents are abusing their children; teenagers are rebelling; kids are running away from home; and the fabric of the family, as we have always known it, is unraveling.

Violent crime is rampant in America. Murder, rape, and robbery are all on the increase. News of bizarre and heinous crimes hardly shocks us anymore. Satanic cults are no longer uncommon. The media report human sacrifices and cultic slayings with sickening regularity.

Our society indulges itself in drugs, alcohol, sex, and entertainment. Substance abuse, rape, murder, suicide, prostitution, and teenage pregnancy are the prevalent problems in our public schools.

We are suffering the consequences of our choices. Is it any wonder that we are raising a generation of children who are hostile to holiness? How can we expect them to love God or the things of God when we have told them there is no God, the Bible is not relevant for today, its standards of morality are outdated, and there is no heaven to gain or hell to shun? Why should they care? They have no fear of God!

AMERICA IS IN TROUBLE

After being elevated to a place of world leadership in a few short years, the United States is now committing moral suicide. It breaks my heart to see where our nation is headed. I am a husband by choice, a father by desire, a preacher by calling, but I am an American by birth. I realize that God is no respecter of persons. He plays no favorites. I know that America is not God's pet, but I also know that no nation could have ever been so prosperous apart from His blessing.

America did not become great because of her vast resources, her superior intellect or determined willpower. America became great because God made her great. Our spiritual heritage reminds us that many of our founding fathers prayed for God's blessing upon this land. They were serious about God and set out to build a society to reflect His nature and character.

But today's Americans have forgotten their heritage. They have sold their spiritual birthright for a mess of secular pottage. Many are quick to explain away the blessings of God as mere chance and circumstance. They want to elevate man above God and human wisdom above His Word.

It is interesting to note that our nation's Declaration of Independence came on the heels of the Great Awakening, when men like Jonathan Edwards and George Whitefield called America to faith in Jesus Christ. During that great revival in the eighteenth century, nearly one-third of Colonial America professed new-found faith in Christ.

God was spiritually preparing America for freedom so we would know how to use our liberty to His glory. Unlike Europe, where revolution often led to unbridled chaos and self-indulgence, the American revolution brought about a glorious display of God's hand in human society. A democratic republic, based upon the moral principles of Scripture, was formed to ensure liberty and justice for all.

In recent generations all of that has changed. America has sown the wind and is now reaping the whirlwind of His judgment. We first began to tolerate sin, then we legitimized it, and now it is flaunted and running unbridled in our city streets.

The Bible tells us in the book of Isaiah, that the evidences of a corrupt society include materialism, corruption, bribes, injustice, lawsuits, dishonesty, greed, and moral perversion. How can anyone look at our society and fail to see the obvious parallel?

The prophet Hosea warned Israel, "Seeing thou hast forgotten the law of thy God, I will also forget thy children" (4:6). America is on a collision course with the judgment of God. Destruction looms on the horizon. No one seems to have a solution to our most serious national problems. The times in which we are living demand God's personal intervention if we are to survive.

JUDGMENT HAS ALREADY BEGUN

We frequently hear it said that if America does not repent, God will have to judge her. However, it is my conviction that God's judgment on America has already begun. Most of us envision that God's judgment will come through some cataclysmic nuclear holocaust. However, God's initial or remedial judgment always precedes His final judgment.

As any society resists God's Word, disobeys His principles, and rejects His authority, God gradually withdraws His presence and leaves that society to its own devices. I believe that process has already begun in America. God is turning us over to the consequences of our chosen path, and we are becoming slaves to our own appetites and victims of our own choices. If we persist in our rebellion, the process will result in final, cataclysmic judgment. But we do not have to experience disaster to reap the initial consequences of judgment.

America, on the one hand, is in danger of turning away from God altogether, like Europe, and developing into a godless, secular society. On the other hand, America may also turn out like Latin America, where people give religion lip service without submitting their lives to its truths. A recent national poll indicated that while most Americans profess to believe in God and the Bible, very few practice what Scripture teaches. Most professing Christians claim they believe the Bible; they just don't want to live by it.

Desperate times call for drastic measures. Radical spiritual surgery is needed to remove the cancer of self-indulgence, arrogance, and complacency that is destroying the very soul of the nation.

Lest we become smug social critics, let us remind ourselves that the sins once peculiar to the secular world have infiltrated and, in too many cases, engulfed our churches and Christian homes. Western Christianity is in serious trouble. We are playing church and losing the battle against evil. In fact, the condition of our society is really no more than a magnified reflection of the condition of the church. It is no wonder that all of our impressive programs are not holding back the flood of moral degeneracy in our society and that we are lagging behind in our efforts to interest a lost world in the gospel of Christ. Judgment must begin in the house of God!

With all my heart, I believe that nothing short of a genuine revival will suffice. Such a revival will restore the Word of God and the God of the Word to their rightful, sovereign place in our national life. Such a revival will expose and cleanse the hypocrisy, shallowness, impurity, materialism, and conflict in our churches and homes and will transform them into holy tabernacles filled with the power and presence of God.

HEARTCRY FOR REVIVAL

During the eighteenth and nineteenth centuries, America experienced genuine spiritual revivals. In each of these centuries, there were visitations of God which awakened the church out of its lethargy and endowed it with new life, love, fervor, and power. Like a great prairie fire sweeping across the nation, the power of God drove back the tide of sin.

Unfortunately, there has been no such revival in America during the twentieth century. God has not seen fit to give a nationwide revival in our time. There have been divine moments here and there, but no outpouring of grace as in centuries past.

With the prophet of old, my heart cries out, "Oh that Thou wouldest rend the heavens, that Thou wouldest come down" (Isa. 64:1). For the past twenty years, I have been privileged to preach revival truths in hundreds of churches throughout North America. Year after year I have listened to pastors pour out their hearts regarding the spiritual needs of their people. I have heard the countless cries of frustrated Christians seeking deliverance from barren, fruitless Christianity.

I have come to the heartbreaking conclusion that something is wrong—drastically wrong. Something is wrong with our view of God. Something is wrong with our view of sin. Something is wrong with our view of the Christian life. We have grown so accustomed to the darkness that we have forgotten the light.

Deep in my heart is the prayer of the psalmist who pleaded, "It is time for Thee, LORD, to work: . . . Wilt Thou not revive us again: that Thy people may rejoice in Thee?" (Pss. 119:126; 85:6).

As I have studied the ways of God in revival, I have become convinced that we do not have to settle for an unrevived condition in the church. God is longing to pour out upon our generation the refreshing, reviving presence of His Spirit. He is longing to set us free to live victorious and abundant Christian lives that glorify Him.

But there are some questions that I believe we must stop and ask ourselves. These questions require serious and honest answers.

Do we really need revival?

I have heard more than one religious leader exclaim enthusiastically, "We are in the midst of a great spiritual revival!" Judging by certain criteria, one might agree with this assessment. After all, a recent Gallup poll indicated that over 60 million Americans claim to have had a "born-again experience." Even the secular press has drawn attention to a so-called resurgence of evangelical Christianity.

Look at the impressive statistics of our Bible-believing churches. "Super churches" with "super programs" abound. We boast the best churches, the best missions programs, the best Christian schools, the best television and radio ministries, the best printed literature, and some of the best preachers that the world has ever known.

But ironically, while we have been offering our "best," we have at the same time experienced a dramatic acceleration of crime, moral perversion, and self-centered, hedonistic living in our society. If the church is so strong and healthy, why isn't it like salt and light, making a greater impact on the world in which we live?

The pure, committed, Spirit-filled lifestyle of the early church caused the fear of God to fall on the unbelieving world. Drawn by the power of the Holy Spirit, quite apart from gimmicks, prizes, and contests, lost people flocked to find the Savior. Could we honestly say that even our biggest and best soul-winning programs are producing that kind of interest?

And look at the quality of those early converts. Luke records that "they continued stedfastly" (Acts 2:42). It didn't take food and entertainment to keep those newly baptized believers coming back to church. Their commitment was to the teaching of the Word, to fellowship and worship, and to prayer. Think of it! Those early followers of Christ would have been hard pressed to understand the part-time, weekend brand of Christianity that we produce today.

If the essence of Christianity is merely knowing the right things and doing the right things, then maybe we're doing all right. But the truth is that God keeps the record book on the heart. He knows how many of us know right and do right, while covering up hearts that aren't right. True spirituality is measured not so much by what we know and what we do (as important as these are), but by what we really are in our inner hearts before God.

We may impress each other by our knowledge of the Bible, but God is not impressed if we fail to be transformed by what we know. I recall one pastor who admitted to me, "I know how to study the Bible to prepare a message, but I don't know how to feed on it to let it transform my own life."

If spirituality can be measured by activity, then perhaps our churches don't need revival. But if it is measured by holiness and purity, then we are woefully in need of revival. When God turns the spotlight of His Word on our churches, we want to paint over our failures, pat ourselves on the back, tell ourselves how wonderful everything is, keep pumping ourselves up in the energy of the flesh, and hope that nobody ever discovers the dead men's bones that lie beneath our beautifully whitewashed spiritual tombstones.

We need to humble ourselves before God, get honest about our true spiritual needs, and fall on our faces before Him in repentance and obedience. Only then can we truly cry out for the reviving and restoring ministry of the Holy Spirit in our lives.

What is genuine revival?

"Revival" may be one of the most misunderstood terms in our Christian vocabulary. Perhaps it would help to establish what revival is *not*.

First, revival, in the biblical and historical sense, is not just a week of meetings. Many churches have meetings without having revival. We cannot schedule revival on our human calendars. Of course, we may set aside a concentrated period of time to seek God, but revival is wholly the work of God, scheduled on His timetable in heaven.

Then, revival is not just excitement or an emotional experience. While revival may be accompanied by both, the fact that the church is jam-packed, that people are ecstatically clapping their hands, or that they are weeping at an altar is not necessarily evidence of genuine revival. Such experiences may be the product of man-made manipulation, or they may be remorse for the consequences of sin, rather than genuine repentance for the sin itself.

Further, true revival is not to be confused with efforts in evangelism. This seems to be the most common misconception of revival. The word "revive" means to quicken or bring back to life. Lost people cannot be revived. They need to be born again and receive spiritual life. Genuine revival normally gives birth to spiritual awakening among lost people and renewed efforts on the part of God's people to evangelize the lost. But revival itself is the movement of God's Spirit in the hearts of His people ("Wilt Thou not revive us again: that Thy people may rejoice in Thee?"—Ps. 85:6).

Richard Owen Roberts, an authority on the subject of revival, has suggested that "revival is an extraordinary movement of God that produces extraordinary spiritual results." It is that divine moment when God intervenes supernaturally in the lives of His people. In fact, ten seconds in the presence of God can accomplish more than all the human effort of all time combined. When revival comes, it restores our first love for the Lord Jesus and brings unquenchable joy in our spiritual service. Revival releases us from the bondage of sin and self, and sweeps us into the freedom of life in the Spirit.

Revival leaves us hungering and thirsting for God. We are no longer satisfied with human efforts, man-made programs, or short-lived strategies. Revival leaves us seeking that which is real, lasting, and supernatural. It causes us to seek the truth, even if it hurts, and it offers permanent solutions, not temporary panaceas.

Revival awakens in our hearts an increased awareness of the presence of God, a new love for God, a new hatred for sin, and a hunger for His Word. Revived believers are no longer content to fill their notebooks and the margins of their Bibles with great insights; they are eager to get the Word into their daily lives. Revival results in a fresh commitment to obey anything God says to us and to yield without question, hesitation, or reservation to the Lordship of Christ in our lives. Intense love for Jesus and increased faith and fervency in prayer are marks of revival. That which before was duty now becomes a delight. Believers who endured religion now enjoy an intimate, fresh relationship with Jesus Christ.

The kind of revival we need will radically change our values, commitments, priorities, attitudes, and relationships to God, to His

Word, and to each other. External conformity to Christianity will no longer suffice. Instead, we will be committed to have the personality, spirit, character, heart, and life of Jesus Christ formed within us.

What is the price of revival?

The greatest cost of revival may be our pride. Are we willing to agree with God about everything He reveals to be contrary to His way? Are we ready to surrender all of our secret, hidden sins and come to the cross in brokenness, repentance, and humility? Are we willing to stop transferring the blame for our problems and take personal responsibility for our own failures?

This process of dealing with sin is a painful one. The Word of God is a sword that cuts and exposes our sinful flesh. But it is impossible to experience spiritual health and the joy of godly living apart from yielding to this ministry of His Spirit.

There are other sacrifices that must be made if we are to see genuine revival. As there can be no childbirth without travail and labor pains, so there can be no revival apart from the labor pains of fervent, persistent prayer. Halfhearted, casual, sporadic, feeble praying will never call down the fire of God's presence from heaven. Isaiah's lament has a tragically contemporary ring: "There is none that calleth upon Thy name, that stirreth up himself to take hold of Thee . . ." (Isa. 64:7).

Lazy, undisciplined flesh would rather feast than fast, play than pray, and watch television than study God's Word. But lazy, undisciplined flesh will never know the times of refreshing found in God's presence.

There have been great revivals without unusual promotion, music, or preaching, but there has never been a mighty movement of God's Spirit apart from extraordinary, sacrificial praying.

You say, the price tag for revival is high. But wait, there may be more. Under the purifying, purging presence of God, He may ask us to relinquish some of our traditional methods and programs that have become empty and useless. I fear that many of us are willing for God to solve all of the problems and conflicts in our churches as long as He doesn't touch our pet programs and established ways of doing things. What if God asked us to dispense with some traditional method or service that has long since become empty and meaningless?

The point is, revival is costly. It cost God His only Son to deal with our proud, stubborn, rebellious hearts. It cost Jesus His life to redeem us from the dominion of sin and self. God's grace is not cheap. The price tag is genuine humility and absolute surrender of everything we hold dear.

But no sacrifice that God might require can begin to compare with the overwhelming, indescribable joy that will be ours when the fog of sin and self is cleared away and we see Him as He really is, in all His holiness, beauty, and radiant glory.

Oh, that we might give Him unreserved permission to have His way. It is time to seek Him with all of our hearts. It is time to prepare in the wilderness a highway for our God. Let us lift up to Him our humble, fervent heartcry for revival before it is too late.

Chapter 2

The Glory Is Departing

As the Nazi armies marched across Europe in the dark days of World War II, one of the leaders of the allied forces lamented, "The lights are going out all over Europe!" The fact was that the spiritual light of the gospel had already been extinguished in the churches of Europe, and the advent of the destruction of human society was inevitable. Whenever any society turns its back on God, it opens itself to a spiritual warfare it cannot survive.

These are dark days in the Western world. The light of the gospel has all but gone out in Europe, and now it is flickering badly in America. Secularism is the religion of our time, and hedonism is the spirit of the age. Sincere and godly Christians are generally viewed as outmoded relics of the past. The preaching of the old-time gospel is decried as out of step with the times.

The social revolution of recent decades has left today's generation cut loose from its moral foundations, adrift on the sea of self-indulgence. Our society is caught up in the pursuit of material things despite the fact that no created thing can bring lasting satisfaction to the human heart. The more we have, the more we want, until our pursuit of prosperity has become the greatest idolatry of our time.

Even our churches have fallen victim to the spirit of the age. Feasting has replaced fasting. Today's church is like a fast-food restaurant with the pastor serving as the cook. We whip in on Sunday, grab a quick meal, and blast off to do what is really important in our lives. The pastor stands there smiling, holding out an offering plate and collecting our guilt-motivated tips. In fact, much of today's Christianity and modern church growth can be explained by human effort, clever marketing techniques, and borrowed money.

You would think if anyone were to call a halt to this ecclesiastical travesty, it would be those of us in the ministry. But not so. Most of us are in a hurry to get going as well. After all, there are people to meet, places to go, and things to do. And where is God in all of this? I'm afraid He is neglected and forgotten in the very place that can least afford the departure of His presence.

"How can you say that?" you may be thinking. "God won't depart from His people. He can't forsake America. We are His last hope to evangelize the world." The problem with this line of reasoning is that it just doesn't stack up with Scripture. God departed from Israel in the Old Testament, withdrew His glory from the temple, and let barbarians destroy it. Who do we think we are that He might not do the same to us?

As I have talked to Christian leaders, pastors, and laypeople about what is taking place in our nation today, I believe there is cause for grave concern. No possible combination of human laws, efforts, programs, or methods can possibly solve the plethora of problems that plague our society. The widespread dishonesty, promiscuity, immorality, self-indulgence, and pride that characterize our godless society stagger the minds of even our finest thinkers.

In the mdist of all this moral chaos and spiritual darkness, today's church seems to have lost her sense of purpose and calling. We are supposed to be the light of the world, but the contemporary church is barely distinguishable from the darkness that surrounds her. We have programs, promotions, seminars, schools, colleges, universities, and television and radio programs to make our jobs easier. But we have become the laughingstock of the world, not because of the offense of the cross, but because of the offenses of believers against the holiness of God. We are impotent against Satan's onslaught. All our programs, methods, and gimmicks have not produced genuine revival.

True revival is that divine moment when God bursts upon the scene and displays His glory. When such a revival occurs, everything that is holy and sacred receives its proper place. When God is enthroned, all else bows before Him and acknowledges Him. It is then and only then that a radical reversal of all our man-made systems of religion will occur.

The problem with American Christianity is that we want to control God instead of letting God control us. We have replaced absolute surrender with conditional commitment to His will. We want to approach God with a carefully detailed contract instead of turning our lives over to Him as a blank check to do with as He wishes.

Revival is not something we can manufacture by human effort or carefully constructed formulas. Revival is that spiritual renewal and reawakening that occur only when God's people repent and surrender to Him afresh. God's plan has always been that His people, enabled by His Holy Spirit, should be different. He wills that we live pure and holy lives in the midst of this dark and perverse world. We are to shine as lights in the darkness, radiating the truth to those enslaved in sin.

But we have failed to fulfill our high and holy calling. We have sacrificed purity and holiness on the altar of pleasure and happiness. It is no wonder that today's church is powerless against the onslaught of evil in our world. While we are playing church, the devil is playing for keeps!

THE NEED FOR REVIVAL

As I study Scripture and the history of the church, I can only conclude that nothing short of genuine revival will spare us from God's judgment. We need true revival—not revival meetings properly scheduled and advertised—but genuine revival in which God's people humble themselves, pray, seek His face, and turn from their wicked ways.

We need to be convicted, cleansed, and transformed by the power of the Holy Spirit, so He can display His glory through us to a lost world that desperately needs His grace.

A self-centered, backslidden church has no interest in evangelizing the lost and no power to be used of God to convict people of their sin. We cannot remain as we are and hope to capture the world for Christ. Only when we adopt the values, priorities, and concerns of the heart of God can we be empowered by His Spirit to fulfill our true calling to be the salt of the earth and the light of the world.

Revival is needed to bring the church back to New Testament Christianity and release the power of God in our nation. Such a revival will sanctify and cleanse us by bringing greater repentance of sin in our lives. It will empower us with the power of the Holy Spirit, not with our clever human devices, remedies, and gimmicks. It will cause our hearts to pursue God with renewed vigor and devotion. And finally, such a revival will give us a new vision for God's work on this earth.

When revival comes it will sweep away all that does not glorify God and will leave us transfixed, focusing on Him and Him alone. The wood, hay, and stubble of human effort will be consumed by the presence of God. Only the gold, silver, and precious stones which are the result of supernatural activity will remain. As God builds His character in His people, He will display the glory of His presence in their lives.

The heartcry for revival was expressed by the psalmist when he wrote, "Wilt Thou not revive us again: that Thy people may rejoice in Thee?" (Ps. 85:6). When God is glorified in our lives, we experience the true purpose for which we were created. Then and only then can we know the power of His presence and the joy of our salvation.

God's glory is the manifestation of His presence. Wherever God is acknowledged, worshiped, and obeyed, He will display His glory. The Israelites in the Old Testament called it the *shekinah* or the glory of Jehovah. Moses saw it and glowed from being in the presence of God. Later the *shekinah* rested on the ark of the covenant in the tabernacle for nearly five hundred years. Eventually, the ark was placed in the temple of Solomon in Jerusalem. There it remained for over four hundred years.

For nearly a millennium, God's glory dwelt with the people of Israel. But there came a time when God withdrew His glory and departed, leaving Israel without hope against her enemies. If America's Christians do not repent of their sins, I fear that He will do the same to us. In fact, God already may be withdrawing from us.

WHEN THE GLORY DEPARTS

Ezekiel, who was both a prophet and a priest, was captured by the Babylonians. He tells us that while he was being held captive, God appeared to him out of a whirlwind in a great cloud of glory and fire, similar to the one which led the Israelites while they journeyed through the wilderness. Ezekiel's vision takes us on a strange journey into the land of Israel as he is caught up by the Spirit of God and taken back to Jerusalem.

The Babylonians had risen to power in the Near East and threatened the kingdom of Judah. Prophets like Jeremiah, Daniel, and Ezekiel spoke out to warn the people of impending disaster if they did not repent of their sins, but the people did not heed their warnings.

Jerusalem was at the brink of disaster. One more act of rebellion and the Babylonians threatened to return and destroy the city and its beloved temple. During the next ten years the people refused to repent and seek the Lord. Instead, they went even further into idolatry and sinful corruption.

Captives, like Ezekiel, hoped for some word of spiritual revival. Perhaps Jerusalem could still be spared, but no word of such a revival ever came to their ears. Instead, the Scripture tells us:

> Moreover all the chief of the priests, and the people, transgressed very much after all the abominations of the heathen; and polluted the house of the LORD which He had hallowed in Jerusalem. And the LORD God of their fathers sent to them by His messengers, rising up betimes, and sending; because He had compassion on His people, and on His dwelling place: But they mocked the messengers of God, and despised

His words, and misused His prophets, until the wrath of the LORD arose against His people, till there was no remedy.

(2 Chron. 36:14–16)

What could possibly have been so bad that there was no remedy? Ezekiel would find out firsthand. God told him that He had set Jerusalem in a strategic place "in the midst of the nations" (Ezek. 5:5). But instead of remaining faithful to God as a witness to those nations, she had changed His commands into wickedness and rebelled against His laws. Therefore, God announced, "I . . . am against thee. . . . because of all thine abominations" (5:8,9).

The Spirit of God then lifted up Ezekiel and transported him to Jerusalem, to the temple. The prophet testified that the glory of God was still there (8:4), but he was shocked to see what else was there. First, he saw a pagan Babylonian idol (an "image of jealousy") at the gate of the altar. Then God tore a hole in the wall of the Holy Place to let Ezekiel see into the house of God (8:7). When the prophet went in, he saw the animal-like "idols of the house of Israel" (the northern kingdom) painted on the walls (8:10). At the door of the sanctuary, he saw women "weeping for Tammuz," an Assyrian goddess (8:14). Finally, he came upon twenty-five men facing east, worshiping the Egyptian sun god (8:16).

I believe God wants to tear a hole in the wall of the church today and expose its sin. We are weak and powerless to stem the tide of secularism because we are not a holy people of God. If we could see into the lives of God's preachers, leaders, and people, we would be appalled. Recent revelations of moral and financial corruption in the lives of some of our prominent spokesmen are but the tip of the iceberg of spiritual and moral decay in our churches.

America is in trouble today because her churches are in trouble. We lack spiritual leadership in this hour of crisis because we lack spiritual leaders. Many of our most renowned preachers are more interested in promoting themselves than Jesus Christ. They are more concerned about their own material prosperity than they are about the spiritual welfare of the church. Tear a hole into the wall of hypocrisy in today's church, and you will see people bowing down to the idols of this century as well.

All of this must have seemed incredible to the prophet Ezekiel. How could the people of Jerusalem sink to such corruption and expect to continue in God's favor? Perhaps they had simply come to take it for granted. Many of them believed God would never allow His temple to be destroyed; therefore, they had a false sense of security. They were trusting in the building and not the Lord. Others knew that the *shekinah* glory dwelt on the ark of the covenant in the Holy of Holies. So powerful was the glory of God that no one dared to look into the ark or even approach it. Even the high priest could only enter the Holy of Holies once a year on the Day of Atonement.

Certainly, Ezekiel must have wondered how God could remain with His people when they had violated His temple so severely. Then something happened that Ezekiel never thought he would see—the glory of God departed! In four distinct stages God's glory lifted from the ark of the covenant (9:3), moved over the cherubim (10:4), departed from the temple (10:18), and finally ascended back to heaven from the Mount of Olives (11:23).

I can just imagine the *shekinah* glory beginning to move from the ark for the first time in a thousand years. Oh, how God must have grieved! Gradually the glory cloud lifted off the wings of the cherubim and began to ascend above the ark of the covenant. Higher and higher it rose until the cloud filled the outer court and then began to drift away from the temple, leaving it empty, lifeless, and dark.

NOBODY NOTICED GOD WAS GONE

Gradually and reluctantly, God departed from Jerusalem, and nobody noticed except Ezekiel. They were all too busy with daily routines, busy schedules, and religious rituals to observe that God had left them. We can only assume that for the next few years, they went right on playing religion without God. Perhaps the high priest lied to the people when he entered the Holy of Holies that year to discover that it was dark and God's glory was not there. After all, he could not tell the people that God had departed. What would they think? So he lied to them and claimed that God was there.

I am deeply troubled that American Christianity is at similar crossroads today. Our churches are filled with the idols of modern civilization. We think we can have all this world has to offer and somehow hold on to God too. While Ezekiel's prophecy was directed to the nation of Israel, which enjoyed a unique covenant relationship with God, it still bears a striking resemblance to the church in America today. The accusations of God's prophet were not levelled against the pagan Babylonians, but against the people of God.

Too many people today are going through the motions of religion without God. We have services, programs, projects, weddings, funerals, and fellowships; but we do not have the presence and power of God. Billy Graham once said that if we took the Holy Spirit out of the church today, 90 percent of all its activities would keep right on going! Much of what happens in our churches can be explained by self-effort, hard work, and psychological manipulation. I will never forget hearing Adrian Rogers say to a conference of four thousand men, "We have no right to be believed so long as we can be explained." Only the unexplainable intervention of God in the hearts of His people can demonstrate His real power to our world today.

The problem is that things are not getting better. Charles Colson said:

> We sense that things are winding down, that somehow freedom, justice and order are slipping away. Our great civilization may not yet lie in smoldering ruins, but the enemy is within the gates. The times seem to smell of sunset.[1]

It is the eerie awareness that the darkness is upon us that concerns today's Christian leaders. Like children afraid of the dark, we want to run and hide from it. But in our fear we forget that our greatest weapon against the darkness is the light of God's Word and the presence of His Spirit in our lives. We, like ancient Israel, have been the receptacles of

His glory because He dwells within us. But somehow like Israel, today's church seems to be losing the glory, and so few are willing to admit it.

The problems facing today's church are not just a matter of a few shysters. I fear we are dealing with a cancerous malaise that is eating away at the very fiber of Christianity. Our condition is deep and serious, and it is not just going to go away. God is departing from our midst for the same reasons He departed from Israel. If we do not repent of our selfishness and wickedness, He will likewise leave us to our own devices until there is "no remedy."

AMERICA: IN A DARK HOUR

Like Ezekiel, the prophet Isaiah who lived a century before him, was never voted one of the "Ten Most Popular Citizens of Jerusalem." He, too, sensed the end was coming for the people of God. More than a century ahead of Ezekiel's time, Isaiah saw the telltale signs that the nation of Israel was in deep trouble and that it was only a matter of time until judgment would fall.

Isaiah was a literary genius and an uncompromising preacher of God's truth. His messages pierced the consciences and confronted the godless lifestyles of his listeners. Although his messages were directed to the people of Jerusalem, they hold powerful warnings for us as well. Isaiah's portrait of the people of Israel bears a striking resemblance to the church in America today.

The accusations of Isaiah's prophecy are not levelled against the pagan nations surrounding Israel, but against the people who belong to God and bear His name. It should come as no surprise that those who have never known God engage in wickedness. But the horror against which Isaiah cries out is that those who are the chosen possession of God so openly rebel against Him.

Hear, O heavens, and give ear, O earth: for the LORD hath spoken, "I have nourished and brought up children, and they have rebelled

against Me. The ox knoweth his owner, and the ass his master's crib:
but Israel doth not know, My people doth not consider."

(Isa. 1:2,3)

Without flinching, Isaiah boldly proclaims the backslidden condition
of God's people:

Ah sinful nation, a people laden with iniquity, a seed of evildoers,
children that are corrupters: they have forsaken the LORD, they have
provoked the Holy One of Israel unto anger, they are gone away
backward. . . How is the faithful city become an harlot!

(Isa. 1:4,21a)

To the undiscerning observer, religion was flourishing in Israel.
Sacrifices and incense were offered regularly. Religious holy days, rituals,
and feasts were faithfully observed. But under the scrutinizing eye of a
holy God, the external mask of piety could not hide the underlying, ugly
reality of sin, idolatry, and rebellion.

The prophet became God's instrument to lift the deceptive mask,
exposing deep rottenness and filth. What emerges is not a pretty picture:

The whole head is sick, and the whole heart faint. From the sole of
the foot even unto the head there is no soundness in it; but wounds,
and bruises, and putrifying sores.

(Isa. 1:5b,6a)

God's grievances against His people are numerous. Perhaps they
are best summarized in chapter 5 of Isaiah's prophecy. This passage
reveals not only God's case against Israel, but also the grave need of
God's people today for repentance and cleansing.

Materialism

"Woe unto them that join house to house, that lay field to field, till
there be no place, that they may be placed alone in the midst of the
earth!" (Isa. 5:8).

Here was a people motivated by temporal gain and material
prosperity. Never content with the provision of their basic needs, their

sights were ever on the accumulation of more and better things. It's not that God objected to their having fine possessions. The problem was in their heart attitude. Their ultimate goal was to exist "alone in the midst of the earth"—to live for self, to be exalted above others, and to escape the burdens and cares of others.

As God's people living in a materialistic, greedy society, we are all too often guilty of the same attitude. Rather than seeking the eternal riches of His righteousness and giving ourselves to meet the spiritual and physical needs of others, our energy is consumed with indulging the appetites of our flesh. We want to be left alone, to add to our grasp more houses, land, stocks, securities, cars, retirement funds, personal luxuries, and conveniences.

Even as Christian leaders, there is often a self-motivated desire to build our own spiritual empires instead of God's kingdom. Many of us are more consumed with building our reputations than we are in building His reputation. We often seek our own glory instead of reflecting His glory. It is no wonder our churches are in trouble today. All too often the church has become little more than someone's personal platform to promote his own capabilities and career.

Hedonism

> Woe unto them that rise up early in the morning, that they may follow strong drink; that continue until night, till wine inflame them! And the harp, and the viol, the tabret, and pipe, and wine, are in their feasts: but they regard not the work of the LORD, neither consider the operation of His hands.
>
> (Isa. 5:11,12)

The hedonistic, pleasure-seeking nation of Israel did not have time to seek after God. They lived only to "please themselves" (Isa. 2:6). Apparently they even entertained themselves with sensual "pictures of desire" (Isa. 2:16). With blithe disregard for the future, they lived only for the here and now.

The affluence of our times has given most people opportunities and possessions their grandparents would never have dreamed possible.

But despite our economic success, the deepest needs of the human heart have gone unmet as men have forsaken the pursuit of God for the pursuit of pleasure.

Perhaps nothing saps more vitality and power from the life of God's people today than this relentless pursuit of pleasure. We have time for television, ballgames, movies, parties, vacations, sports, and magazines. But we can't find time to pray, to study God's Word, to discipline our lives, to serve the Lord, or to witness for Him.

We are so busy trying to have fun that we have forgotten God. Happiness has replaced holiness as the ultimate goal of God's people. The pursuit of pleasure has replaced the passion for God which once characterized the powerful American church during past days of revival and renewal.

Rebellion

"Woe unto them that draw iniquity with cords of vanity, and sin as it were with a cart rope" (Isa. 5:18).

The picture here is one of open, blatant rebellion. God's people do not even attempt to hide their sin because they have no sense of shame. Rather, they thrill to display their wickedness, dragging it through the streets for all to see.

How the heart of the Savior must grieve to see His blood-bought bride enjoying and flaunting every conceivable sin. Years ago, certain sins were not even discussed among professing Christians. Today, however, the church has little sense of shame over sin. Many of our finest churches are tolerant of the sins of the heart (pride, jealousy, bitterness, envy, and even hatred) as well as the sins of the flesh (adultery, pornography, worldliness, and divorce). I can remember the day when people would not think of telling an off-color joke in front of a minister or a woman; now it is the women and preachers who are telling the jokes!

God help us if our own leaders do not repent and return to the Lord and submit to His righteousness as the standard for their lives. We cannot continue in spiritual rebellion against everything that is holy and sacred and expect to get away with it. One Christian leader said that if God does not judge America, He will have to apologize to Sodom and Gomorrah!

Relativism

"Woe unto them that call evil good, and good evil; that put darkness for light, and light for darkness; that put bitter for sweet, and sweet for bitter!" (Isa. 5:20).

Through repeated disobedience, the conscience of the nation of Israel had been seared; God's people developed a twisted, perverted sense of right and wrong. They could no longer discern between good and evil. They indulged in the things God hated and scoffed at the virtues God loved.

No one can argue that our nation has adopted values and standards contrary to those of God. Hands that shed innocent blood are an abomination to God, yet our courts protect the "right" of a mother to take the life of her unborn child. God resists the proud heart, but our society encourages ladder climbing, self-assertion, and the independent, self-sufficient spirit. God's design for the family calls for submission and yielding of rights, but we demand rights for all. Men have defaulted from leadership in the home, and now women are walking away from their responsibilities as well.

Sometimes the church is also guilty of promoting a way of life which opposes God's standards. God exalts the humble and the poor in spirit, but we boast of our spiritual achievements, our offerings, our church attendance, our programs, our Bible knowledge, and our spiritual maturity. God hates those who sow discord among the brethren, but we delight in broadcasting and publishing the shortcomings and failures of other believers. God hates divorce, but we have found every conceivable reason to justify it. God has established clear qualifications for spiritual leadership. We often ignore those standards and instead exalt men to positions of leadership based on their education, their social status, or their charisma and natural ability. In many ways we have drifted far from the standards of a holy God.

Pride

"Woe unto them that are wise in their own eyes, and prudent in their own sight!" (Isa. 5:21).

In their pride and arrogance, the Israelites had become blinded to their true spiritual condition. They held an inflated view of themselves. They could not see the foolishness of their so-called wisdom.

How like so many of us as believers. We have the answer to everything. Just ask us! Our shelves are filled with notebooks on everything from "How to Have the Perfect Family" to "How to Build the World's Greatest Sunday School." The only problem is we haven't learned how to live in a holy, humble relationship with God and with others.

We are too proud to admit our real spiritual needs. We don't want anyone to think our marriage is struggling, our children are rebellious, or our walk with God is shallow or empty. We go out of our way to hide our sins rather than confess them. We spend greater effort to cover our sins than it would take to deal with them and forsake them.

THE WAGES OF SIN

Written into the constitution of God's universe are certain laws, among which are the consequences for sin. These laws are universal in their application. No one is exempt from the natural consequences of rebellion against God. Israel was no exception. Isaiah graphically and vividly described the price she had to pay for her disobedience:

- The land was overthrown by strangers (1:7).
- Her cities were burned with fire (1:7).
- God rejected her sacrifices (1:11).
- God refused to hear or answer their prayers (1:15).
- God forsook those who had forsaken Him (2:6).
- Their society collapsed into poverty and ruin (3:1).
- There was a dearth of spiritual, political, and social leadership (3:2–4).
- God's people were abused, and the poor were oppressed (3:15).

When the Babylonians destroyed Jerusalem, they tore it down stone by stone. They wrecked the temple and burned it to the ground, but it did not really matter because God had already departed. God is not the curator of some ancient museum. He is not a collector of old religious shrines. He has allowed the enemies of His people to destroy the tabernacle and two temples to emphasize this point. God is far more concerned about the inner sanctuary of the human heart than He is in any building made with human hands.

Today's church is in trouble just as ancient Israel was in trouble. We are reaping many of the same consequences in our own society. We cannot impact society because we are not willing to live holy lives that can convict the godless and draw them compellingly to Christ. We lack great spiritual leaders with the moral vision and spiritual passion to call us to revival.

Several years ago the late Dr. Martyn Lloyd-Jones, that great British evangelical pastor, said, "I am profoundly convinced that the greatest need in the world today is revival in the church of God."

The powerful American preacher Vance Havner has said, "Only a mighty moving of the Spirit can clear the scandal and strife in the church today."[2] In response to the question of whether we were seeing true revival in the churches today, Havner observed that if we were, there would be a spiritual awakening; the divorce rate would drop; pornography, public nudity, and sexual immorality would not be tolerated; lawlessness and crime would decline; and worldliness would be kicked out of the churches. The great problem of our time, Havner observes, is that "the world and the professing church first flirted with each other, then fell in love, and now the wedding is upon us."[3]

IS IT TOO LATE?

In spite of the hardened, idolatrous ways of His people, God revealed Himself not only as a just and vengeful God, but also as a merciful, long-suffering God of covenant love. With eyes of faith, Isaiah saw a Savior who would one day take on Himself the full fury and wrath of a holy God against sin. Mercy was abundant and available, if God's people would only meet His conditions.

Return to God's Word.

"Hear the word of the LORD . . . give ear unto the law of our God" (Isa. 1:10).

We are caught up in the feel good craze of our times. The "psychologizing" of the church has led many to propose every possible excuse for not obeying the Word of God as the ultimate and final authority in our lives, but its truth alone can set us free from the consequences of our sin. Only by complete and absolute obedience to the Word of God can we find hope for the future.

Repent of all known sins.

"Wash you, make you clean; put away the evil of your doings from before Mine eyes; cease to do evil" (Isa. 1:16).

There can be no true revival apart from genuine repentance. Those who want to reduce the gospel to mere easy believism have cut the very heart of conviction out of its appeal. We cannot, we dare not come to God clutching our sins if we are to take hold of His grace. Only as we kneel in repentance before the cross of Christ will we find deliverance from our sins.

Restore Christ to His rightful place as Lord.

"Come ye, and let us walk in the light of the LORD . . . Learn to do well; seek judgment, relieve the oppressed. . . . If ye be willing and obedient, ye shall eat the good of the land" (Isa. 2:5; 1:17,19).

Israel received the glorious promise that God would restore His presence and His glory in "every dwelling place" and in the "assemblies" of His cleansed people (Isa. 4:5). God assured them that He would be for them a place of refuge, protection, and security (Isa. 4:6) if they would acknowledge His rightful authority over their lives. Only when we submit to His authority and Lordship can we hope to be truly free.

The same God who offered spiritual healing and forgiveness to stubborn, rebellious Israel, stands waiting to offer it to us as well. He alone can send times of refreshing to our churches, our homes, and our land. We can experience a great outpouring of His power if we will humbly agree with Him about our need, seek His mercy, and return to Him with all our hearts.

Chapter 3

Where Are the Prophets?

The Marines' idea of looking for "a few good men" is not original. It was God who first said, "I sought for a man . . ." (Ezek. 22:30).

Throughout the history of His dealing with this planet, God has been seeking for men that He could trust—men through whom He could accomplish His purposes.

God chooses different kinds of people to accomplish His purposes. He uses teachers, counselors, helpers, servants, and administrators to edify and build His church. But one of God's keys to dealing with His people has always been His prophets. Historically, prophets are those preachers of righteousness who stand uncompromisingly for the truth of God's Word. They quickly call us to accountability and personal holiness. These servants of God are unashamed to stand against the tide of unbelief, and they are unafraid to point the finger of conviction and say, "Thou art the man!"

Unfortunately, the modern evangelical church in America lacks such people. Few and far between are the genuine prophets of God in the church today. Whether they serve as pastors, evangelists, or missionaries, their motivational spiritual gift is to declare the absolute and certain truth of God's Word both to the Christian community and to the lost world. For the prophet, the Word of God is like a fire raging within his soul. A prophet cannot merely sit back and watch the world go to hell. He must speak up and warn the wicked of their ways and call the prodigal back to God.

In the Old and New Testaments alike, the prophet had a unique place in the ministry of God's Word to His people. Because of the nature of his calling, the prophet often found himself at odds with sinful society. Prophets were often unpopular, and even our Lord Jesus said of Himself that a prophet is without honor in his own country (see Matt. 13:57).

One spiritual gift seems lacking in today's evangelical churches—that of the prophet. We have an abundance of teachers, exhorters, rulers, givers, mercy-showers, and servants, but we do not have revival! Perhaps that is, in part, because of the absence of prophets who fearlessly and uncompromisingly proclaim our need and call the church to repentance. Seminars on revival will not produce revival. Lectures on the history of revival will not produce revival. Lessons on how to have revival will not produce revival. Genuine revival will come only when men and women are convicted of their sins, repent, and turn to God. There can be no real revival without repentance in response to an awakened conscience about personal sin.

Our churches today have bigger buildings, bigger budgets, better methods, and better staff. Our buildings are full to the brim with activity and excitement, but we do not have revival! I believe God is looking for men who will sound the trumpet, show His people their sin, and unflinchingly cry out for a return to the God of our fathers.

Before we can hope to see any significant change in American Christianity, we must have more true prophets of God willing to call us back to holiness—the only acceptable standard for serving God. We need men and women who are willing to let God have absolute authority in their lives. Only then will we be able to witness the powerful influence of lives totally dedicated to the kingdom of God and to the spreading of the gospel of Jesus Christ.

BECOMING USABLE

The prophet was often called the "man of God." His life was characterized by total devotion to God. While the prophets were not perfect by any means, they were more God-like in their character than any of the kings, rulers, or priests because they had no institutional interest to serve. They were solely God's men, and they knew it.

Perfect Heart

God is looking for men and women with a "perfect" heart. "For the eyes of the LORD run to and fro throughout the whole earth, to shew Himself strong in the behalf of them whose heart is perfect toward Him" (2 Chron. 16:9a). These are people who have the rare quality of wholeheartedness, single-mindedness, and genuine sincerity. The prophets of old were ablaze with God's glory. They did not come representing themselves. They came representing God alone. They feared only Him and, therefore, were fearless in their preaching.

The church today is spiritually anemic. We have a high view of ourselves but a low view of Jesus Christ. We set our spiritual standards low, then struggle to meet them, and congratulate ourselves thinking we have done a good job. We tend to magnify the good while tolerating the evil within our own churches. We brag on the choir, the bus ministry, the fellowship dinners, and all our overcrowded schedules, but have little to say about the spiritual depth of our people.

God is not looking for better programs. He is looking for better men and women whose hearts are wholly His.

The awakening in Wales was born out of the ministry of men and women whose hearts were perfect with God. Men like F. B. Meyer and Evan Roberts were the prophets God used in that day to revive His church in one of the few great revivals of the twentieth century.

The Bible urges us to be single-minded in our devotion to God. It also warns that a double-minded man will be "unstable in all his ways" (James 1:8). Unstable men are driven by impulse, circumstance, or the fear of others. But those with perfect hearts have set their minds, wills, and affections on the one supreme objective—to know, love, honor, serve, and obey God with all their hearts. Such wholehearted devotion will not flirt with love of money, self, pleasure, or the praise of men.

Charles Wesley said it this way:

> Oh, for a heart to praise my God,
> A heart from sin set free,
> A heart that always feels Thy blood
> So freely shed for me.
>
> A heart resigned, submissive, meek,
> My great Redeemer's throne;
> Where only Christ is heard to speak,
> Where Jesus reigns alone.
>
> A heart in every thought renewed,
> And full of love divine;
> Perfect, and right, and pure and good,
> A copy, Lord, of Thine!

Purpose and Commitment

God is looking for men and women of purpose and commitment who know whose they are and where they are headed. Such individuals have a sense of direction and are able to provide sound leadership to others. They are driven, not by dreams of grandeur, public acclaim, having their name in print, or being materially secure. Rather, their values and decisions are determined by the ultimate purpose to which they have committed their lives—to be like Jesus and to be pleasing to Him.

Those who understand God's purpose for their lives do not drift through life, waiting for things to happen to them. They do not spend their lives in an easy chair with their feet propped up, one eye on the sports page and the other on the latest prime-time rage.

Their lives are under the control of the Spirit, who makes their days purposeful, their minds disciplined and clear, and their spirits alert, sensitive, and energized by God Himself.

Such people are more concerned about building God's reputation than their own. They are committed to building His kingdom rather than seeking a personal following of their own. Their focus is not on security in this life, but on one day hearing their Master say, "Well done, thou good and faithful servant." That is what gets them out of bed in the morning and keeps them headed in the right direction.

Principles and Priorities

God is looking for people of principle whose lives are governed, not by preference, but by conviction. These individuals will not compromise and cannot be bought. Their choices are rooted in firm, scriptural convictions. They do not do what comes naturally or what is easiest for their flesh. They deny themselves and their fleshly appetites to take up their cross and follow Christ. Their consciences are sensitive, and they know how to distinguish between right and wrong. They "abhor that which is evil; [and] cleave to that which is good" (Rom. 12:9). They are willing to risk their reputation and what others may think of them in order to take a stand for what they know is right.

God is also looking for men and women whose priorities are spiritual and whose values are eternal. These folks know what really matters in life and are willing to make the tough choices necessary to work those priorities out in their daily lives. They are willing to say "no" to many things that are good, so that they can say "yes" to those things that are best.

Men and women of principles and priorities are willing to sacrifice personal comfort and convenience in order to concentrate on those things that matter most in life. Such individuals are not inclined to put their roots down too deeply, for they are looking "for a city which hath foundations, whose builder and maker is God" (Heb. 11:10).

This unwavering commitment to principle is particularly important in the lives of those who would be God's instruments to speak to the church in our age.

Rarely has there been a revival that has not stirred up great opposition, both from the lost world and even from within the body of Christ. When people are exposed for what they really are, if they are unwilling to bow to the truth, they will generally attack and discredit in order to justify their own disobedience.

They will find any number of things to criticize—the length of services, the style of preaching, the personality of the preacher, or methods that may be used. It is at this point that many men in leadership are tempted to back down. They do not want to risk rocking the boat. Rather than being willing to stand and take their chances with God, they succumb to pressure to protect their reputation and secure position. God usually asks us to yield to Him the last ounce of our pride, position, and reputation before He pours out the reviving power of His Spirit. Are we willing to pay such a price?

Purity and Perception

God is looking for men and women of purity whose lives are blameless and beyond reproach. These people take seriously the commands of God's Word to "cleanse ourselves [of] all filthiness of the flesh and spirit" (2 Cor. 7:1). They believe holiness is not outmoded or old-fashioned. They are known at home and at work for their integrity and keeping their word.

My prayer for my life is not that I will be rich or famous, but that I will be holy. My prayer for my sons is that they will be holy men of God who are ablaze with His glory.

It is important to remember that purity begins in the heart. Words and actions are merely external expressions of what is in the heart. In a world that exalts greed and lust and rejects that which is wholesome and good, those of us who long to be used by God must exercise constant care and vigilance to keep our hearts pure.

The one who is committed to personal purity will have a God-given perception. In ancient Israel it was said of the men of Issachar that they "had understanding of the times, to know what Israel ought to do" (1 Chron. 12:32). Men and women of purity are also known for their clarity.

In recent years I have been shocked by the number of Christians who have confessed to me their sin of lust expressed through pornography. I have heard many confess that they have been in bondage to moral impurity throughout most of their adult lives. I know of no sin that will do more to deaden a man's spiritual vitality than the sin of moral impurity.

The one for whom God is looking is willing to deal ruthlessly with every form of impurity in his life. He will not tolerate the smallest compromise. "For this is the will of God, even your sanctification. . . . For God hath not called us unto uncleanness, but unto holiness" (1 Thess. 4:3,7).

To be pure as He is pure means to be able to stand before God unashamed and give an account for every word, thought, motivation, and deed. "Who shall ascend into the hill of the LORD? or who shall stand in His holy place? He that hath clean hands, and a pure heart . . ." (Ps. 24:3,4). "Follow . . . holiness, without which no man shall see the Lord" (Heb. 12:14).

The battle for purity lasts a lifetime. "Keep thyself pure," Paul exhorted young Timothy (1 Tim. 5:22). Such a commitment to constant purity demands a day-by-day surrender to the Holy Spirit's control. Self-effort and self-determination alone cannot keep us from sin. Only God's grace can sustain us against our own vulnerability.

Prayer and Power

God is looking for men and women of prayer, for such people also possess spiritual power. In a day when justice and truth had failed in Israel, the Scripture tells us that "[God] saw that there was no man, and wondered that there was no intercessor" (Isa. 59:16). Tragically, the nation of Israel faced impending disaster because there was no one left to pray or intercede on her behalf.

Charles Finney called prayer the "essential link in the chain of causes that lead to a revival."[1] Sammy Tippit has observed that in every era of spiritual darkness and apathy, God has stirred the hearts of His people to pray for revival.[2] Prayer is the recognition of our utter hopelessness apart from God. We must pray because we are otherwise powerless to stem the tide of evil in the world.

Prayerless preachers cannot move the hearts of people, let alone move the heart of God. When Jesus' own disciples had failed miserably in their efforts to cast a demon out of a young boy, He told them, "this kind goeth not out but by prayer and fasting" (Matt. 17:21). Only with a great effort of prayer can men of God expect great power in their ministry.

STAYING FAITHFUL

Many a child of God has started well, but has failed to remain on course in his service to God. Too many times we forget the commitments and sacrifices that got us started, and at some point in our ministry we decide to coast along and soon fall prey to the schemes of the devil. It doesn't have to happen to us, but we dare not think that it cannot happen. Only when we realize the power of the enemy will we counter him with the weapons and resources God makes available to us. Whenever we substitute human reason for divine revelation, we are bound to fail in the area of faithful spiritual leadership.

The Minister

Spiritual leadership is a divine calling. It is an awesome thing to have been chosen, not by men, but by God, to represent His heart to those under our influence and authority. This calling is a sacred trust, and the consequences of violating that trust are severe. James says that we should not grasp for a leadership position knowing that those of us who teach others shall have the more severe judgment (James 3:1). You see, like begets like. Leadership is a determinative function, and we have to live with what we produce.

I am driven by the realization that one day I will have to give account to God, not only for every aspect of my own life and ministry, but also for the lives of those who were under my leadership (Heb. 13:17). Living in the light of that final judgment motivates me on a daily basis to say "no" to sin and the lusts of my flesh, and to say "yes" to the indwelling Spirit of God.

One of the problems today is that we have exalted men and women to positions of leadership on the basis of their training and education, their natural gifts and abilities, or their money and influence rather than on the basis of scriptural qualifications. These standards certainly ought to be true of every believer, but they are not an option for those of us in positions of leadership. Somehow we circumvent the clear stipulation of Scripture that leaders must be blameless and above reproach and that they must have their own spiritual lives in order.

You see, the things people value simply do not impress God. I am convinced that the apostle Paul could not have made it past the credentials committee of the average church! We are impressed by fancy degrees, great intellects, physical appearance, persuasive eloquence, and natural charm. But God is looking for something else: humility, sincerity, and brokenness.

One of the most important qualities God looks for in our lives is *genuineness.* This is what Bill Gothard and others call a "Life Message." The genuine preacher speaks out of his own life, not just his college or seminary notes. It has been said that "a message prepared in the mind reaches minds; a message prepared in the heart reaches hearts; but only a message prepared in the *life* will change lives." Paul did not say to the Corinthian believers, "Follow my tape library," or "Follow my outlines." He said, "Be ye followers of me, even as I also am of Christ" (1 Cor. 11:1).

Years ago, when I was ordained, I promised God that by His grace I would never preach anything that was not real in my own life. That has often limited the number of messages I could preach! But to preach one inch further down the road than what I am living is nothing short of phoniness and hypocrisy, and it sets me up for a fall.

I have become increasingly burdened about the widening gap between the messages preachers preach and the lives they live. Public revelations of the misdeeds of highly visible Christian leaders have merely served to pull back the curtain on a host of lesser-known leaders who, likewise, are preaching one thing and living quite another. While this hypocrisy occasionally takes the form of a blatant scandal, it is the less-publicized sins of the heart that cause most of us to pollute the temple of God today.

I think of pastors who admitted to me that they rarely take time to read the Bible except to prepare their sermons. Some even acknowledged that they get their messages from other preachers' printed sermons and rarely read the Bible even for sermon material. I think of widely-read Christian authors whose books on marriage and family life belie their own broken vows and their failures as mates and parents. I think of countless Sunday School teachers, deacons, elders, and church staff members who acknowledged to me that the impression others have of them is far different than what is really true. Their private lives are often in spiritual shambles, while their public ministry leaves the impression they are godly examples to be followed.

It is not just others who lack genuine integrity. Each of us must ask ourselves if we are in danger of *talking* further down the road than we are actually *walking*. I preach earnestly against pride, but I would be less than honest if I did not admit that the pride of my flesh daily wages war against the life of the Spirit within me. It is easy to tell others to be humble, meek, and mild while remaining selfish and demanding to those who are closest to us.

Genuineness of heart and life is indispensable to an effective, powerful ministry.

I think of the story in 2 Kings 4, where the woman ran to Elisha and pled with him to come and help her son who had suddenly become ill and died. You remember how Gehazi, Elisha's servant, ran on ahead of his master, perhaps thinking to himself that this was his big chance to establish his own reputation and to make a name for himself. When he arrived at the home of the dead boy, Gehazi went into the room and placed Elisha's staff on the lifeless body. However, lifeless staffs cannot produce life, especially when they are held in the hand of a man who is motivated by personal gain rather than genuine spirituality. Not until Elisha entered the room and literally laid his body, arm to arm, leg to leg, and face to face on that child was the boy restored to life.

The lifeless corpses of those around us will never be restored by empty, lifeless programs, methods, publications, counselors, or messages. We must learn to lay down Spirit-filled, holy, genuine, compassionate lives on others, in order that the life of God may flow through us to them.

In a wonderful treatise on the effective minister and ministry, Paul recounts his labor among the Thessalonians: "For our gospel came not unto you in word only, but also in power, and in the Holy Ghost, and in much assurance; as *ye know what manner of men we were among you* for your sake. . . . Ye are witnesses, and God also, how holily and justly and unblameably we behaved ourselves among you that believe" (1 Thess. 1:5; 2:10 italics mine).

The man or woman who has been entrusted by God with a position of spiritual leadership must minister out of the reality of a pure life. Paul wrote to another church that it was essential for those who served in the gospel to "[give] no offence in any thing, that the ministry be not blamed: But in all things approving [commending] ourselves as the ministers of God" (2 Cor. 6:3,4).

In addition to a holy, genuine life, I believe *humility* is another essential characteristic of a spiritual leader. There is an ever-present danger inherent in becoming successful, as the world or the church measures success. It is all too easy to begin to believe our fans! The more God uses us to reach and touch and bless other lives, the more vulnerable we become to pride.

I have also discovered that the higher we go in authority, position, or influence, the easier it is to become self-deceived and to be blinded by our pride. We begin to think subconsciously that we are the exception to God's rule, that we can do no wrong, and that we speak for God. Well-meaning friends, followers, and subordinates often feed our pride by exalting us beyond what is proper and by telling us only what they think we want to hear. At this point we virtually force God to bring us down, so that He will not be robbed of the glory that belongs solely to Him.

Because of the supernatural revelations he had received from God, Paul was given some sort of impediment to protect him from spiritual pride (2 Cor. 12:7). Though he was a man mightily used by God, he insisted, "I will not dare to speak of any of those things which Christ hath not wrought by me" (Rom. 15:18). He never ceased to be amazed that God could use him! "For I am the least of the apostles, who am not worthy to be called an apostle, because I persecuted the church of God. But by the grace of God I am what I am . . ." (1 Cor. 15:9,10 NKJV). "Unto me, who am less than the least of all saints, is this grace given, that I should preach among the Gentiles the unsearchable riches of Christ" (Eph. 3:8).

We leaders must be willing to pay the price of transparent honesty before those we are responsible to lead. Seldom does a family, congregation, or ministry deal more thoroughly or brokenly with their sin than their spiritual leaders are willing to do.

Truly humble leaders can afford to be honest, transparent, and real with their followers. They do not have to pretend to be something they are not. They do not bristle or become defensive when challenged or questioned. They are teachable and willing to learn, even from their critics. They walk with God and it shows.

The Motivation

Men may measure and applaud visible results in our ministries, but God is equally concerned with *why* we do what we do. I believe that a false standard for measuring success in ministry has put a lot of pressure on us to perform for the wrong motives. Since success is often measured in terms of "nickels and noses," or budgets, baptisms, and buildings, it is easy to fall into the trap of working to impress men with our success in these dimensions. Motives are tricky things, and it is tough to be totally honest with ourselves about them.

There is a desperate need for leaders in the church today whose ministries are more than the sum total of their natural abilities, efforts, and energy. It seems to me that even non-Christians could build the kinds of ministries we often see today, given the right combination of promotion, public relations, fund-raising, organizational ability, and natural leadership qualities. But those who utilize natural means to build their ministries will be limited to natural, explainable results that will burn as wood, hay, and stubble when tried by fire.

We need men and women who recognize that apart from the resurrection power and life of Jesus operational within them, they can do nothing . . . individuals who are utterly dependent upon the power of the Holy Spirit to produce supernatural, eternal results in their lives. People can manufacture the spectacular, but that which is genuinely spiritual can only be produced by the Spirit of God.

The apostle Paul was acutely conscious of the danger of seeking to impress men. He wrote: "For do I now persuade men, or God? or do I seek to please men? for if I yet pleased men, I should not be the servant of Christ" (Gal. 1:10). "Wherefore we labour [are ambitious], that . . . we may be accepted of [well-pleasing to] Him." (2 Cor. 5:9).

Those who live for the praise of men tend to become kingdom-builders. They often manipulate and use people for selfish ends. I must always ask myself the question, "Am I seeking to be recognized and to build a successful reputation, or do I desire only to make Him known?" I have discovered that most of us as preachers are really very insecure. We allow ourselves to be imprisoned by others' expectations and perceptions. We are afraid of failure, and we are desperate for the acceptance and approval of others. Therefore it is quite natural for us to do whatever is necessary to impress others.

However, the fear of man always brings a snare. Our own insecurities can drive us to be motivated to impress, please, or be accepted by others. When that becomes our driving force, we are no longer able to boldly proclaim God's truth—especially when it is not palatable to our hearers. I believe this is at the root of why so many pastors are afraid to confront, expose, or deal with sin in their churches. They want to be liked and accepted! They have fallen into the trap of becoming men-pleasers rather than God-lovers.

The true servant of God fears God rather than men. He is driven by a desire for God to be glorified and His kingdom to be built. He uses his ministry to build the lives of people rather than using people to build his ministry. He has a servant's heart. He does not seek personal gain and is willing, whenever necessary, to limit his own freedom so as not to damage other lives or restrain the message he proclaims.

When Paul went to Corinth, he refused to take an offering, though he certainly had the right to have his material needs met by those to whom he ministered. But he did not want anyone to be able to accuse him of being in the ministry for personal gain (1 Cor. 9:6–15). His heart is expressed in the words, "I seek not *yours,* but *you.* . . . And I will very gladly spend and be spent for you . . ." (2 Cor. 12:14,15 italics mine).

Paul's deepest motivation was expressed to the Thessalonians: "But as we were allowed of God to be put in trust with the gospel, even so we speak; not as pleasing men, but God, which trieth our hearts. . . . Nor of men sought we glory, neither of you, nor yet of others . . ." (1 Thess. 2:4,6).

The Message

The message that has been entrusted to ministers of Christ is a sacred gospel. Paul called it "the glorious gospel of the blessed God, which was committed to my trust" (1 Tim. 1:11). He challenged young Timothy, "Study to shew thyself approved unto God, a workman that needeth not to be ashamed, rightly dividing the word of truth" (2 Tim. 2:15).

As in the early church, there are many so-called ministers of the gospel today who have perverted and prostituted the truth of God's Word and have led perhaps millions of people into a doctrinal abyss. Both Peter and Jude warned about these false teachers whose message denies the Lordship of Christ, who promote fleshly indulgence, sensuality, and rebellion against authority, and who teach that "gain is godliness," all under the guise of preaching the gospel.

The Scripture warns against false teachers, saying, "Their mouth speaketh great swelling words, having men's persons in admiration . . ." (Jude 16). "While they promise them liberty, they themselves are the servants of corruption" (2 Peter 2:19).

God's servant will teach people how to discern between truth and error, so that they will not be swept away with every wind of doctrine. He will proclaim the "whole counsel of God" ("I kept back nothing that was profitable unto you"—Acts 20:20), including those aspects of God's truth that are not palatable to the flesh. He will not hesitate to lay down, as Jesus did, the claims of true discipleship or to call people to deny themselves, take up their crosses daily, and follow Him.

The message of the cross is an affront to the pride and self-sufficiency of the natural man. Down deep he wants to believe that he can make it on his own and that he really does not need God. When our Lord laid down the terms of true discipleship, the Bible tells us that "many of His disciples went back, and walked no more with Him" (John 6:66).

In the Old Testament the men with the greatest following were usually false prophets who fed the people what they wanted to hear. The true prophets, those who spoke for God, were seldom popular, but they were not running for office. They were not trying to move up their denominational ladder; they were not afraid of losing their retirement benefits; no headquarters pulled their strings, except heaven.

It is also important to remember that the message we proclaim is the truth. With Him there "is no variableness, neither shadow of turning" (James 1:17). Therefore, we must make sure that all of our communication is completely truthful. Paul could state, "We spake all things to you in truth" (2 Cor. 7:14).

Preaching the truth is what the ministry is all about. It is our only message to declare to a lost world. Therefore, we dare not deceive our listeners with distorted truths, inflated statistics, inaccurate facts, or even use selective texts to support our own preconceived notions or to defend our own lifestyle preferences.

The apostle Paul said of his own ministry, "For our exhortation was not of deceit . . . nor in guile" (1 Thess. 2:3). Therefore, he explained: "[We] have renounced the hidden things of dishonesty, not walking in craftiness, nor handling the Word of God deceitfully; but by manifestation of the truth commending ourselves to every man's conscience in the sight of God" (2 Cor. 4:2).

The Method

The clear teaching of God's Word is that we must use holy means to obtain holy ends. Not only was the ark of the covenant sacred, but the men who carried it, the poles on which it was carried, and the means by which it was carried, all had to be according to God's precise instructions. Failure to carry it God's way (even by sincere, well-intentioned men) resulted in more than one death.

Once again we must ask ourselves, "What is my purpose for being in the ministry?" If my purpose is to build a big church, then I will use whatever means are at my disposal for filling the auditorium. But if my purpose is to glorify God by building a holy church, then I will use means designed to accomplish the objective.

In this entertainment-crazed generation, we have become far too dependent on celebrities, gimmicks, promotions, contests, and giveaways to build our ministries. Whatever happened to dependence on the ministry of the Word, prayer, and the power of the Spirit?

Ours is a day when the end justifies the means in the church as well as in the world. Therefore, it is tempting for Christians to rationalize that adopting the culture of the world will better enable us to reach the world. But I am convinced that the world is unimpressed with a religious version of itself. Only a holy church with a holy message and holy methods can ever truly win the world.

The New Testament states that many people followed Jesus for all the wrong reasons: multitudes, miracles, and meat (see John 6). But when our Lord insisted that they submit to Him as Master, many of them turned away. It is not difficult to *attract* people to magnificent auditoriums with star-studded programs, but our real task is to *attach* them to the Lordship of Jesus Christ. In order to do so, our lives, our message, our motivation, and our methods must reflect the values of the kingdom of God, not the philosophy of this world.

Above all else, it is required that we be found faithful. I think of the Old Testament account of the twelve priests entrusted by Ezra to take gold and silver to the temple in Jerusalem. Before they left Babylon, Ezra carefully counted, weighed, and measured the precious vessels, and then instructed the priests, "Watch ye, and keep them, until ye weigh them before the chief of the priests . . . at Jerusalem, in the chambers of the house of the LORD" (Ezra 8:29).

Upon arrival in Jerusalem, the twelve priests delivered their treasure to the priests and Levites, who once again weighed all the vessels to be sure nothing was missing. Those twelve men succeeded in their mission, even against difficult odds and obstacles along the way (Ezra 8:31), because they knew they would have to give account once they arrived in Jerusalem.

You and I have been entrusted with the priceless treasure of the gospel of Jesus Christ. We must guard it carefully. The day is soon coming when we will stand before our Great High Priest and give account of our faithfulness to the ministry to which He called us. We must be faithful when no one but God is watching. We must be faithful in obscurity as well as in publicity . . . in times of adversity as well as in times of prosperity.

The One who has called us is faithful and true, and He has said, "Be thou faithful unto death, and I will give thee a crown of life" (Rev. 2:10). Oh God, give us such men and women today!

What's Gone Wrong?

Part Two

Chapter 4

What Have We Lost?

Bill and Kerry were a typical American couple when they walked into our crusade in a large church in the Bible Belt. They appeared outwardly successful to everyone around them. They seemed to have it all—jobs, money, success, and prestige. They were living the American dream. The only problem is the dream was more like a nightmare for them.

"We were both so busy all the time," Bill said, "that our jobs drove us apart. I was chasing the almighty dollar and neglecting my wife's personal and emotional needs."

"I was way over-committed," Kerry acknowledged. "I was working nights and Saturdays. We were never together, except on Sundays."

"We were faithful church-goers," Bill admitted. "But we sat there empty inside. We had the best money could buy, but we didn't have each other. Our schedule was so bad that we almost never had time for each other."

"It wasn't long until I found myself turning to someone at work for emotional support," Kerry confessed. "It all started so slowly that I rationalized the whole thing. 'I just need somebody to talk to,' I would tell myself. But as time passed I began to feel the guilt of hiding this emotional affair from Bill."

As they drifted further apart, Bill and Kerry became critical of each other. Little things that used to be accepted became glaring points of confrontation. She began criticizing him excessively because of her own guilt over her relationship to the man at work.

"She kept screaming at me, but I wasn't hearing her heart," Bill acknowledged. "I couldn't figure out what was going wrong. I had no idea what the root problem was, and therefore, I had no idea how to meet it."

In time, Kerry broke off the relationship with the man at work. But things did not improve in their marriage because she was carrying guilt so intense that it was like an invisible shield between them. In time, Bill also turned to someone at work for the emotional support he felt he needed. But after four months, he ended that relationship because of his own guilt. He wanted to confess this to Kerry, but he believed Satan's lie that "if I get honest, she will reject me."

For four years they plodded on in their relationship without ever turning to each other or the Lord. Their once vibrant Christianity was an empty shell of what had once been. All the power of Christ was gone. They were going through the motions of religion without a relationship that could sustain them.

"I guess I just told myself that I would have to live with the consequences of my mistake," Bill said.

"I did not know what he had done," Kerry explained, "and he did not know what I had done. I, too, decided to bury it and try to go on, but I was miserable and restless inside."

"During the Life Action crusade at our church, I came under deep conviction that I needed to clear my conscience with Kerry," Bill said. "I finally realized that my guilty conscience was the barrier that stood between us."

"I was under conviction also," Kerry explained, "but I was afraid that if I told Bill the truth, he would divorce me. I kept trying to rationalize that I needed to keep quiet in order to keep our marriage together for the sake of our children."

When they both decided to be honest with each other, Bill and Kerry went for a drive, parked the car, and began to talk.

"I thought I really knew him," Kerry said, "and I never expected that he, too, had been unfaithful."

"We were both afraid to get honest with each other, but honesty was exactly what we needed," Bill explained.

"Once we honestly confessed to each other, it was like the burden of the world was lifted away," Kerry added. "It wasn't easy to hear, but the honesty and clearing of our consciences that resulted brought a fresh, new vitality to our marriage and to our spiritual lives."

"After the initial shock," Bill added, "we got down to the business of rebuilding our marriage and our lives. We both decided that we would rearrange everything and realign every priority to protect our marriage and our walk with God."

"God gave us both the grace to forgive each other and to reach out to each other," Kerry stated. "We began to fall in love all over again like newlyweds. Suddenly our emotional bonding grew stronger. We were emotionally and physically attracted to each other like we had not been for years."

It wasn't long until Bill and Kerry's relationship was so improved that they became secure in each other's love, and once that happened they were able to reach out to others and minister to them. In time, Kerry quit her job and they cut back their expenditures so they could live within the salary Bill was making.

"We had less money," Bill observed, "but we were happier because we were spending less money too. We put God first in our lives and our marriage and family next, and everything else took a back seat. It was amazing to see the turnaround that resulted."

"We were excited to go to church," Kerry explained. "We couldn't wait for the next service. We were right with God, He was blessing our lives, and it was the greatest feeling in the world."

God transformed Bill and Kerry when they admitted what was wrong and sought His forgiveness and restorative power. Like many Christians today, they were going through the motions of playing church but they had lost the power of God in their lives. They had no desire to reach out to others because, first of all, they needed to reach out to Him.

POWERLESS CHRISTIANITY

The church is waiting for the world to come to Christ and get saved, but the world is waiting for the church to come to God and get right. God does not judge a nation simply because of the wickedness of the ungodly. He also judges a nation because of the disobedience of His own people. Without the power of God in our lives, we have nothing to offer this world that can really make a difference.

Jesus put it simply: "Without Me ye can do nothing" (John 15:5). Without His life operationally living through us, the sum total of everything we can do that has eternal value is zero. It does not matter how many seminars, insights, formulas, ideas, or programs we have been exposed to; we cannot succeed in the Christian life without God. No one can live the spiritual life apart from the power of the Spirit.

All the cosmetic improvements in the world will not empower us to live for God. The only person who ever succeeded in living the Christian life was its author, Jesus Christ. The only way you or I can hope to live like Him is by going to the cross and exchanging our lives for His life. We can wear our best clothes, be on our best behavior, and even talk our best talk to impress others, but none of that impresses God! God is only impressed with the sinless life of His Son. Unless His life is released in us, all else is vain.

Even full-time Christian workers often miss this point. We can get so busy in the work of the Lord that we forget all about the Lord of the work. He is the whole reason and purpose for our existence. When we overlook Him, we lose the refreshing power of His presence in our lives. To compensate for the barrenness inside, we keep up the facade of religious activity on the outside. The result is always spiritual burnout. We become tired of the treadmill and weary in the work. First, we lose the power of God, then love and joy go. Soon peace is gone, and it isn't long until nothing is left. That's when we begin enduring Christianity instead of enjoying Jesus, its author.

Do you remember what it was like when you first got saved? Many of us were overwhelmed with the realization of what God had done for us. We were wonderfully conscious of the presence and power of God in our lives. We were so in love with Jesus that we didn't need worldly pleasures to fill the void in our lives. We were so excited about the Bible that we didn't need television. We were immersed in spiritual things, and talk of God punctuated everything that came out of our mouths. Christ and Christ alone was our joy of living.

Have you ever noticed that it is usually the new converts who experience such joy and excitement in their relationship to God? They come to church and actually expect to hear from God! They sing the hymns as if they really mean what they are singing; they can't keep tears from flowing down their cheeks when people talk about spiritual things. They want to give witness of their new-found faith to everything that moves. You say, "Give them a few months, and they'll get over it." They will, if they sit next to most of us!

What happens to these joyous, fresh, new converts? What has happened to many of us? In many cases, these young believers begin to realize that the older converts don't share their excitement. In time, the new believers also lose their power and joy. The thrill they once knew diminishes. The motivation disappears and the zeal erodes.

Loss of spiritual power does not necessarily begin with a flagrant act of sin. It may start with slothful, undisciplined habits. Like the glory of God gradually, reluctantly departing from the temple, God slowly withdraws the manifestation of His presence. Chances are, we haven't openly rebelled against God. We are too spiritual for that. We just let Him slip away a little at a time until we feel empty inside. But even then we are too proud to let anyone know that we are slowly dying spiritually.

LOST AXE HEADS

I have always been struck by the story of Elisha's disciples ("sons of the prophets") who went to the Jordan to cut wood to build a new dwelling place. The story is recounted in 2 Kings 6:1–7, where we read:

> But as one was felling a beam, the ax head fell into the water: and he cried, and said, Alas, master! for it was borrowed. And the man of God said, Where fell it? And he shewed him the place. And he cut down a stick, and cast it in thither; and the iron did swim. Therefore said he, Take it up to thee. And he put out his hand, and took it.
>
> (vv. 5–7)

When the disciple lost the axe head, he lost the power that went with it. He was now helpless to complete his task. In desperation he turned to Elisha to help him, and the prophet's miracle of the swimming axe head recovered it for further use.

I believe this story has some striking parallels to the Christian life. We might say that the axe handle represents all that you and I are, apart from Christ—all of our natural abilities and efforts. The axe head, on the other hand, represents the supernatural power and presence of the resurrected Christ in our lives. Too many of us have lost the axe head and are attempting to accomplish the work of God with a useless axe handle! We are as busy as ever, but all our busyness is not necessarily godliness. We are engaged in activities, plans, and programs of every kind. But if God is not in them, they are powerless.

The greatest tragedy of our time is the powerlessness of the modern church and of the average Christian. We have lost our power with God and, therefore, we have no power in the world. We are consumed with activities, but we are not consumed with God!

Can you imagine what our world would be like if the manifest presence of God touched down in the church today? Can you imagine what would happen in America if God moved upon the church from the Atlantic to the Pacific, from the Gulf of Mexico to the Canadian border? If a revival were to break out today of the magnitude of the Great

Awakening in the eighteenth century, over twenty million Americans would be swept into the kingdom of God!

That kind of revival will not happen as long as we spend our time and money building bigger buildings, sending out more evangelists and missionaries, increasing our efforts at higher education, and developing more programs. All those things alone are simply no substitute for the power of God.

How is it that God's people lose their spiritual power and influence? What goes wrong, and what can be done to prevent it or get it back? In my own life, I have discovered three specific things that most often cause me to lose the presence and power of God in my life.

Pretense

Pretense may be the greatest hindrance to revival in the church today. We have so much material prosperity and technological equipment that we can appear to be spiritually successful even when we are not. Phony Christians go through the motions of their religion every Sunday. They attend church, slap the preacher's back, sing the songs, put money in the offering, and go through all the motions. This is not only true in liberal churches but in our fundamental and evangelical churches as well. In many cases, today's Christianity is nothing more than a cosmetic paint job on a broken piece of equipment. It looks good, but it doesn't run.

I am convinced that millions of professing Christians are just going through the motions. They live one way six days a week and put on Christianity for two hours on Sunday morning. They know the jargon and the clichés. They even know how to look Christian, but they are just pretending. They are talking further than they are walking with God.

I remember hearing about a clown who lost his job at one circus and applied at another. He was told there were no openings for clowns but that they needed someone to dress up like a large monkey to entertain the spectators. The clown agreed to take the job and discovered he was good at imitating a monkey. People could not tell the difference between him and the real monkeys. He chattered, ate bananas, and swung on the ropes to the crowd's delight.

Next to the monkey cage was a lions' den. Soon the clown discovered that the more he swung on a rope over the lions' den, the more the crowd roared with glee. Being an entertainer at heart, he became more and more daring. One bright Saturday afternoon, he was in his heyday, thrilling the crowds that had gathered. He swung way out over the lions' den, and all of a sudden the rope snapped. He landed right in the middle of that den of lions. Those lions began to roar and stalk and paw the costumed clown. Terrified, he ripped off his monkey's hat and began to yell, "Help! Help! Get me out of here!"

Just then, one of the lions looked at him and said, "Shut up, man; we'll all lose our jobs!"

That is how it is in too many of our churches. We are just playing at Christianity, and we have even succeeded at deceiving ourselves. How often do our families battle each other all the way to church, only to walk in the door with a fake smile and pretend everything is fine? We sit complacently for an hour or two then smile at everyone as we walk back to our cars where all-out war begins again on the way home.

Another believer says to us, "How are you doing?" And what do we say? "Fine." Fine? Are we really? We're dying inside, we're angry at our mate, we're in bondage to moral impurity, we're head over heals in debt . . . . But we're *fine?*

Several years ago, I conducted a staff revival for a Christian organization. After three days the associate director of the ministry asked if he could share something with the entire staff. Before he began to speak, he just stood there for a moment. Then he leaned his huge frame on my shoulder and began to weep uncontrollably. When he finally spoke, he said, "I've preached for ten years. I've travelled all over the country. I know all the answers, principles, and formulas, but I'm empty inside. I feel like a big empty pipe with a bunch of nuts and bolts rattling around on the inside. I'm empty and I'm sick of it. I can't go on like this."

Then he just cried for the next several minutes. As he sobbed, I realized God was flushing ten years of pretense out of his life. As I looked at the other staff members, I asked, "Do you know the only difference between Bill and most of the rest of us in this room? He finally got honest enough to deal with his need, and the rest of us are still sitting here pretending!"

Then I said, "I want to ask those of you who would be honest enough to admit that you are just like Bill to get up out of your seats, go to Bill, and ask him to pray with you." Without hesitation two-thirds of that staff got up and went to Bill's side. Then I suggested that they get together as a group each morning to pray and ask God to fill their empty lives and make them spiritually real. They called it the "Empties" class!

Several weeks later, I called and asked Bill how the "Empties" class was going. "Great!" he said. "But we don't call it 'Empties' anymore because we are all getting filled to overflowing!"

Pride

Pride is another thing that will cause us to lose the presence and power of God in our lives.

Pride is thinking we are better than God knows we really are. It causes us to make ourselves the exception to the rule. It feeds on self-gratification, self-satisfaction, and self-promotion. Pride causes us to think that what we know in our heads, we actually have in our lives. This is one of the great weaknesses of today's church. We have more information than any generation in church history, but we lack the depth and character of previous generations. The more we know, the more we think we have accomplished. But in reality, spiritual lethargy, deadness, and barrenness are the real trends of our time.

"I" trouble is ruining modern Christianity: "I know this," "I've done this," "I've been there," and "I've seen it all." This subtle, but hideous pride of self is killing modern Christianity. We think we are really something, when the Bible says we are nothing without God.

The very attitude that says, "I don't need revival," is generated by pride. Pride of knowledge, pride of position, pride of possessions, pride of achievement, etc., fills our hearts and squeezes God out of the picture. After twenty years in the ministry, I am convinced that pride is the root problem of all other sins among God's people. Pride causes us to avoid repentance and run our own lives without God.

Pride causes us to want to deal with the respectable rather than the real. Pride feeds the attitude that says, "I have to keep up a good front" or "I don't want to get *that* honest." How many times have you sat through testimony meetings at church and thought, "When are these people going to get real?" Rarely do we hear people openly admit their real needs. Someone will say, "Pray for me that I'll be a better husband or father." That's a nice, respectable prayer request.

When was the last time you heard somebody say: "God has convicted me that the reason I'm not a good husband or father is because I'm in love with myself. I love myself more than my wife or children or even God. I love television more than His Word. I love indulging my flesh more than building my spirit. In fact, my whole world revolves around me. I'm sick and tired of my selfishness. Please pray that God will change my heart."?

Pride causes us to deal in generalities rather than specifics. Our tendency is to lump our confessions together in such a way that we don't have to deal with any specifics. Most of us would rather pray, "Oh God, forgive all my sins," than "God, forgive me for being a liar, a cheat, a thief, a gossip, or a rebel." We don't like getting that specific with God.

That same pride causes us to want to view our sins as simply problems, mistakes, or weaknesses. Jesus did not endure the torture and condemnation of the cross for our "problems." He didn't die just for a few character flaws. He died for our sins. Only His shed blood can overcome the sin in our lives.

Pride causes us to be more concerned with what people think about us than what God knows about us. The greatest hindrance to revival in most of our lives is pride. It keeps us in our seats when we ought to be on our knees. Pride says, "Don't go forward in the service. After all, what will people think!" Pride freezes our response to spiritual conviction. It keeps us from confessing, "I was wrong." Pride is the reason most of our kids never see us on our knees except when we're adjusting the color on our television sets!

Pride causes us to be satisfied with things the way they are. It causes us to live independently of God rather than depend on Him. That is why it is the height of arrogance to think we don't need revival.

Years ago, while I was preaching in Hattiesburg, Mississippi, my wife, Judy, and I went to dinner with the associate pastor and his wife. He was a sanguine, jovial person, and we found ourselves telling jokes and stories and laughing together and having a good time. There was nothing wrong with any of it, but that kind of situation easily feeds our pride. Soon I found myself trying to top each story with a funnier one.

It wasn't long until I found myself exaggerating one of my stories. God immediately convicted me that exaggerating is really a respectable word for lying. I knew that I ought to confess what I had done to the couple we were with, but pride said, "It's just a little thing. Forget it." That night I couldn't sleep; I was miserable. When I arrived at the church the next day, I felt like I had lost my "axe head." The sense of God's presence and power in my life had departed. I couldn't preach until I found that couple and confessed what I had done. As soon as I asked their forgiveness, my conscience was clear, the glory of God was restored in my life, and I was able to preach with freedom and power.

Personal Disobedience

Nothing robs us of the power of God faster than personal disobedience to God's commands. Disobedience says, "no," when God says, "go." It keeps us from doing what we ought to do with the right heart attitude. Disobedience says, "I'll go this far but no further." It limits God's power in our lives.

Whenever we disobey God, we lose the axe head of His power. Samson toyed with temptation until he finally laid his head in Delilah's lap and got a haircut in the devil's barbershop. He lost the power of God in his life. The Bible says, "He wist not that the LORD was departed from him" (Judg. 16:20). The problem with sin is first it thrills, but then it kills. It blinds and binds its victim.

I am convinced that today's church is blinded by pride. Many professing Christians merely go through the motions of Christianity. They pretend to be happy when they are really empty, miserable, and powerless.

You and I cannot excuse disobedience in our lives. No one is the exception to God's rules. Fallen preachers, broken commitments, and damaged testimonies are all too often the norm rather than the exception in today's evangelical churches.

RESTORE THE JOY

The vital question is, how do we get the power of God back in our lives? People often say to me in frustration, "Del, I've tried everything and I still don't have the power." The problem is that God does not ask us to *try* but to *die*. Only when we die to ourselves can His power replace self-effort in our lives.

That prophet who lost his axe head had three options. First, he could quit. And that's exactly what all too many disillusioned believers today have done. They've simply given up.

Second, he could fake it. I can just imagine those other prophets watching their friend trying to chop wood with nothing more than an axe handle. He's out there working up a sweat from early morning till late at night. Bark is flying everywhere. Everyone is impressed with this hard worker. But no trees are falling.

Isn't that a picture of so many of us? We're busy, busy, busy. But we're also barren inside. Someone has said, "Busyness produces barrenness." That is often true. But in my life, I have discovered that "barrenness produces busyness." Some of the busiest people in our churches are simply covering up for the lack of inner reality and power in their lives. That's why they have to work so hard, to make sure nobody finds out what they're like inside.

Third, he could go back and retrieve the lost axe head. And that is exactly what we must do when we have lost the presence and power of God in our lives.

Notice what happened to the young prophet. First, he cried out for help. Until we acknowledge our need, the power of Christ will never be restored.

Second, he went to his master. His master was Elisha; our master is Christ, and He is the only one who can meet our needs.

Third, he returned to the place where he lost the axe head. We, too, must go back to the place where we lost the power of God in order to recover it. Where is it that you lost His power? At what point did pretense, pride, or personal disobedience cause you to lose the axe head? Identifying the cause of our barrenness is essential to restoration.

Fourth, God performed a miracle and caused the prophet's axe head to float to the surface. Perhaps you are thinking, "I've gone too far. I could never again experience the fullness of God in my life. That would take a miracle!" My friend, God has performed a miracle for you. Even as Elisha cut down a stick, cast it into the waters, and the iron axe head surfaced, so 2,000 years ago, God cut down a tree and hung His Son on it in order that you and I might know the miracle of restoration.

Finally, Elisha said to the prophet, "Take it up to thee—Reach out and take it!" Most of us are waiting for God to move on us in some traumatic flash. But while we wait for God to fall from heaven, He waits for us to fall before Him. The next move is yours. God is right where He has always been. He is simply waiting for you to come back to Him. Reach out and take His presence and power. It's yours!

Chapter 5

When Are We Going to Get Honest?

Forrest and Linda Lowry are being used by God today to touch the lives, marriages, and ministries of hundreds of people. Forrest was pastoring the Spring Baptist Church near Houston, Texas, when he invited us to conduct a revival crusade in his church. By all outward standards, they were a successful couple with a very successful ministry. In reality, they were hiding behind masks of pretense until they humbled themselves before God and their congregation.

Listen, as they tell their story in their own words.

Forrest:

At thirty-nine years of age, after preaching for twenty-three years, I found myself pastoring a large, successful church (as the world measures success). But inside, I was hollow and defeated.

Much of my life, I had been on a spiritual roller coaster. Periods of victory were soon followed by defeat. It seemed that the defeats were becoming more common than the victories. Since my teenage years, I had periodically struggled with lust, which had been fueled by an addiction to television programs and movies that I had no business watching. This caused tension within my marriage, which robbed us of the joy of physical intimacy.

I had become an absentee father. My children were receiving my reactions to their wrong choices but not the loving instruction they needed. I remember threatening my family with resignation from the church because they were not living out the things I preached from the pulpit. I didn't realize that my precious children and wife were merely a reflection of my own disobedience.

At the root of all the surface symptoms, my heart was filled with pride. I would not agree with God about my sin, and I certainly did not want anyone else to find out what I was really like. So I lived in pretense—going through the motions, but with little reality or power.

I reached a point where I believed I was doomed to this lifestyle. I honestly felt there was no hope. Thank God I was wrong.

Prior to the crusade, I began to pray and ask God for personal revival. It all began with the fresh work of God in my wife's life. I am so grateful she had ears to hear and eyes to see what her need was and that she chose to do something about it. As she began to come alive, God brought real conviction to my heart. As God changed her, He removed one of my lame excuses for my own defeat. She was not the problem—I was!

Finally, I became desperate for Him to work in my life. That's when He began to speak to me through His Word about my choices. I was so excited because I had wondered if He would ever really speak to me again. I will never forget going to the prayer room during the crusade and writing out a personal commitment: "I choose *brokenness* (God's will, not my will). I choose *humility* (I agree with God and will not think more highly of myself than He actually knows and will not attempt to cause others to think better of me than God knows to be true). I choose *obedience* (to do what God says, when He says it, with the right heart attitude)." This was not an emotional experience. I was simply ready to make the right choices. And my life has not been the same since!

This led to an honest confession before my wife, children, church staff, and ultimately, the church, of my past condition and my new choices. I no longer had a reputation to maintain with pretense. I was free to live honestly and transparently, without fear of what others thought. God's Word came alive! My marriage was restored. My children began to confess areas of sin in their lives. I experienced real freedom over the sin of lust. Preaching has become a joy, as I am motivated to share the truth of God's Word, out of the reality of my own experience.

Please do not misunderstand me. There are still daily choices to be made. Wrong choices are possible, but choosing brokenness, humility, and obedience can be the habit of my life. "I do not regard myself as having laid hold of it yet; but one thing I do:

forgetting what lies behind and reaching forward to what lies ahead, I press on toward the goal for the prize of the upward call of God in Christ Jesus" (Phil. 3:13,14 NASB).

Linda:

God found me burned out as a pastor's wife and a Christian. I was so tired of trying to live the Christian life in the energy of my flesh. I was a pretty good imitation, but in my heart I knew I was a fake, giving lip service to the Lordship of Christ. My heart had grown cold and calloused. I couldn't fake being a happy Christian any longer. I started looking for an escape. The cry of my heart was, "Oh that I had wings like a dove! for then would I fly away, and be at rest" (Ps. 55:6).

I sought escape through sleep, having been addicted to over-the-counter sleeping pills for five or six years, through hobbies, counted cross stitch, reading novels and magazines, soap operas, and television—anything to fill the void so I wouldn't be confronted with the barrenness of my life.

My husband, knowing that I was miserable and depressed, tried to help me, but Satan had convinced me that my husband really didn't understand me or even care. I started blaming him for my misery and the shallowness of my life. I thought that if *he* were different, then I would be different, and our marriage and ministry would be different. I started living in a "dream world," imagining what it would be like to be out of my marriage, and seriously entertained thoughts of divorce.

Finally, I became desperate for God to do a work in my life, for I knew if He didn't, there was no reason for us to be in the ministry. As I called out to Him, even in anger, He heard and answered.

He began by showing me the truth about my life, which enabled me to stop blaming my husband for my condition. He showed me that my anger and bitterness toward my husband were really saying, "God, You made a mistake in the person You gave me for a husband." My pride made me think I deserved better.

As God searched my heart, showed me my sin, and I agreed with Him about my sin, I literally came to life again. God revived my heart. He filled my life with His joy, love, and peace, and gave me a new desire to spend time with Him in prayer and in His Word. He delivered me from years of resentment toward my husband and gave me a brand new perception of him and an incredible new love for him.

As I laid the sleeping pills on the altar, God graciously and miraculously delivered me from the bondage that had made me a prisoner for years. I could lie down and sleep at night knowing that God was the giver of sleep and not depend on the pills that had so controlled me.

God has truly transformed my life. He has replaced despair with hope. How I praise Him for His patience and loving-kindness toward me, and for a new husband, a new marriage, and a new ministry.

A song that was sung during the crusade in the church, beautifully expresses the new song that God has put in my heart:

"Jesus will set up His Kingdom within you,
Filling the void with delight,
Taking dominion over selfish desires,
Transforming the darkness into light,
Transforming the darkness to wonderful light.

"When His Kingdom comes, what a difference;
When things are in earth,
As they are in heaven;
When all has been settled
And my heart is His home,
Oh, what a difference,
What a great transformation!
When His Kingdom comes."[1]

SPIRITUAL NAKEDNESS

Most of us are familiar with the story of "The Emperor's New Clothes." He had been deceived by his tailor, who told him that only the most wise and intelligent people could see and appreciate his new robe. Not wanting to admit his own ignorance, the proud monarch paraded around stark naked, thinking he was really impressing everyone. Because of his position, no one wanted to speak up and embarrass him, so they pretended to believe the whole charade.

Finally, a little boy, who didn't know any better than to tell the truth, shouted out that the king had no clothes on, and the crowd finally got honest and began to laugh with the little boy.

Unfortunately, that is how a lot of our modern evangelical churches are today. We parade around in all our spiritual nakedness, priding ourselves on what a great job we are doing. As God has shown me the reality of my own needs and the wonder of what could be ours through Christ, I have often felt like that little boy. I want to cry out against the pretense and hypocrisy of it all, not because I am any better than anyone else, but because I am convinced we all must be honest with God and ourselves if we are to have any hope of recovering His glory and power.

THE COST OF DISCIPLESHIP

There has always been a theological debate over the relationship of salvation to discipleship.[2] While much ink gets spilt, few Christians really come to grips with the seriousness of the issue. Jesus Himself made it crystal clear that discipleship is tantamount to professing faith in Him. There is no such thing as being saved but unwilling to become a disciple. Those who want to make discipleship a secondary aspect of sanctification have missed our Lord's whole emphasis on what it means to be a disciple.

Discipleship is not optional! It is the requirement of all who profess faith in Jesus Christ. The term *disciple* means a "disciplined one." The disciple was not merely a learner in the sense of a student. He was more than that. He was to be disciplined to the lifestyle of his master. Thus Jesus took the disciples with Him to teach them, both by His words and His example.

Our Lord did not set up a school, purchase desks, prepare lessons, and hand out diplomas. He went far beyond that by exposing His life and character to His disciples. He wanted them to be like Him by allowing Him to transform them.

Jesus was not content with mere outward professions of faith. At the height of His popularity, He rebuked many of His would-be disciples for following Him for all the wrong reasons (see John 6:1–71).

Some people were drawn to Jesus by the multitudes that thronged Him. As long as He was the local hero and a resounding success, they followed Him. Others flocked to Jesus because of His miracles (6:2). After He fed the five thousand (6:9–15), they flocked to Him for the meat He could provide.

But when Jesus began to proclaim Himself as the Master and to lay down the demands of true discipleship, many of the masses changed their minds. From that point, the Bible tells us in John 6:66, "many of His disciples went back, and walked no more with Him." What did they indicate? That they did not really believe in Him! Genuine belief and true discipleship were equated as one and the same by our Lord.

When Jesus turned to the Twelve, He asked, "Will ye also go away?" (v. 67). But Peter responded, "Lord, to whom shall we go? Thou hast the words of eternal life. And we believe and are sure that Thou art that Christ, the Son of the living God" (vv. 68,69). Unlike those who followed Him for the wrong reasons, His true disciples acknowledged Him as their Master.

If the contemporary church in America is to have revival, we must remove all hypocrisy and pretense; otherwise, we are no better than the soldiers who mocked Jesus, saying, "'Hail, King of the Jews!' And they smote Him on the head . . . and did spit upon Him, and bowing their knees worshiped Him" (Mark 15:18,19). We are no different than they if we claim to worship Him while rejecting His claim of Lordship over our lives.

Jesus commented on this kind of hypocrisy when He quoted the prophet Isaiah (29:13), saying, "This people draweth nigh unto Me with their mouth, and honoureth Me with their lips; but their heart is far from Me" (Matt. 15:8). Our Lord preached the necessity of true discipleship and thinned out His crowd. We are afraid to preach His message because we are so desperate to build our crowds.

Just as the religious leaders of His day were upset with Jesus' preaching, so many are disturbed by the preaching of the true gospel today. Easy believism has become the curse of the modern evangelical church. We want converts so badly that we have failed to ask them to repent of their sin and truly commit themselves to Christ's authority and Lordship.

THE MISSING INGREDIENT

I have spent much time over the years trying to understand and account for the bland, explainable brand of Christianity that seems to be the rule rather than the exception in so many of our churches. Where is the joy, the vibrancy, the enthusiasm, the supernatural, the enormous impact on society that characterized the early church? Must we be content with a religious experience that is routine, usual, average, and void of the miracle-working power of God's Spirit?

Almost every day I meet believers who endure a roller-coaster Christian experience. You know what I mean: up one day—down the next. For a while they're excited about walking with God and serving Him. Then they go through a period of disinterest, coldness, and defeat. Up and down . . . up and down. Why?

For too many Christians, a consistent and fruitful spiritual life is an elusive dream. A few still hold on to the hope that some day they will find a magical spiritual formula and everything will be different. Unfortunately, however, I fear most Christians have quietly resigned themselves to this less-than-ideal state, deciding that "nobody else seems to be doing any better. I guess this is the way it's going to be until we get to heaven." So they hang on and hope for the Rapture.

It's time to call a halt to the merry-go-round of humdrum Christianity. It's time to pull the switch that operates the roller coaster of up-and-down Christianity. It's time to say to the riders of both these games, "You don't have to keep going 'round and 'round and up and down! You can get off these painful rides that you keep calling the Christian life!"

You see, unless God has died and His Word is a lie, then the Christianity described in the New Testament is still available to those of us who live in twentieth-century North America!

If this is true, what is the missing ingredient in Western Christianity? I believe there is one thing missing that can make all the difference in the world. The missing ingredient is commitment. Apart from genuine commitment that arises from deep within our hearts, there is no way to

73

escape the monotony of the religious merry-go-round or the agony of the spiritual roller coaster.

I can already hear some of my dear friends thinking, "Well, lack of commitment is certainly not my problem. If anything, my problem is over-commitment. I'm committed to more activities and responsibilities now than I can handle. You should see my schedule! I'm obviously committed."

Let me hasten to say that I am not speaking of commitment to programs and organizations. What I believe must be addressed is the matter of a fundamental, underlying, nonnegotiable surrender to the Lordship of Christ and the authority of Scripture.

This commitment must supersede and govern all other commitments and involvements. Once this basic surrender is made, a multitude of daily decisions and struggles may be eliminated. This deep-seated, lifetime commitment settles, once and for all, all future decisions. Years ago, one of our staff expressed it this way to me:

> As a child, I made a lifetime commitment to the Lordship of Christ and the authority of Scripture. I bowed my will and acknowledged Him as my only Lord and Master, and myself as His servant forever. In effect, I said to God, "Whatever You say to me for the rest of my life, I will obey You without hesitation, questions, or reservation." I committed myself to obey Him whether I felt like it or not, whether it was easy or not, whether it made sense to me or not, whether anybody else agreed or not.
>
> That moment of unconditional surrender has been the driving force behind my living and decision making every day since. Now when I am faced with a temptation to pamper my flesh, to ignore the promptings of God's Spirit, or to disobey His clear instructions, I don't have to struggle. That decision was made the moment I committed my life to His Lordship.

There is a sense in which this commitment is like going on a diet. There are two basic approaches to dieting. One is to say, "I really need to lose twenty pounds; I really shouldn't eat any more sweets." This dieter has set himself up for failure, because every time he is faced with a dessert, he will battle within himself: "That looks delicious. But it's got a zillion calories in it! But I haven't eaten anything sweet since yesterday. But you'll gain weight if you eat it." More often than not, our overweight friend is likely to give in to the cravings of his appetite.

On the other hand, the successful dieter determines what is necessary to lose weight and begins his diet with a commitment. For example, his commitment may be that he can't eat any desserts. If he is serious about his commitment, he will not have to struggle every time a dessert is passed his way. His decision has already been made. Based on his initial commitment, he simply says, "No, thank you!"

The heroes of Scripture who were victorious over sin and self were men and women who based their lives on a commitment. Why was Daniel able to refuse the king's delicacies and persist in public prayer when he knew it might cost him his life? He had purposed in his heart that he would not defile himself and that he would be a faithful worshiper of Jehovah. No earthly monarch could dissuade him from his commitment to the King of heaven.

Joseph refused to be seduced by Potiphar's wife. He preferred to be deprived of his liberty than to break his commitment to obey the authority of God's law.

No indication is given that Shadrach, Meshach, and Abednego wavered for even a moment in their determination not to bow down and worship King Nebuchadnezzar's likeness. They knew the consequences for their insubordination. But they had already counted the cost.

Why was Paul willing to be shipwrecked, beaten, and falsely accused throughout his entire earthly ministry? Years earlier on the road to Damascus, he had made a commitment from which he could not be swayed. It became the basis for every aspect and decision of his life.

Let me make a few observations about this commitment.

Conscious Choice

God abhors all attempts to straddle the fence or to be a middle-of-the-roader. As an eleven-year-old I know once said, "If you sit in the middle of the road, you're going to get run over!" Time after time God has drawn the line and challenged His people to consciously choose a life of commitment to Him. The only alternative is a life of rebellion against Him. There is no middle ground. Joshua put it this way: "Choose you this day whom ye will serve" (24:15). Elijah was adamant: "How long halt ye between two opinions? if the LORD be God, follow Him: but if Baal, then follow him" (1 Kings 18:21). And Jesus confronted the church: "I know thy works, that thou art neither cold nor hot" (Rev. 3:15).

Total Commitment

I cannot hold on to something else and say that I am truly committed. So many of us wish to profess commitment to Christ but also keep something to fall back on. Genuine commitment necessitates burning every bridge behind us. Then in times of pressure, there will be literally no turning back. Could this be why Jesus told the rich young ruler that he must give up all his possessions before he could become a disciple? Jesus knew the one area of his life that young man was unwilling to relinquish. Until his fist was unclenched and all his rights and assets were released, he was still living under his own lordship and was not ready to acknowledge Christ as Lord of his life.

First Kings 19 paints a graphic picture of total commitment. Elijah went to call Elisha to be the next prophet of God. As a symbol of his wholehearted surrender to God's call, Elisha took the oxen with which he had been plowing his field, killed them, and boiled their flesh. He made a public statement that he would never (and could never) return to his old way of life.

This is the commitment Jesus asked from His disciples when He called them to leave their nets and follow Him. However, after the crucifixion of Christ, Peter got discouraged. He made the tragic mistake of returning to his nets. When Jesus appeared on the shore early the next morning, it was to ask Peter to reaffirm his basic commitment: "Peter, do you love Me more than all of this . . . Then follow Me!" (see John 21:15–19).

Lifetime Surrender

The Old Testament illustrates total commitment with the concept of a bond servant. Under the law, a master could not own a slave more than six years. In the seventh year, all slaves had to be released. However, a special provision was made if a slave loved his master and wished to make a voluntary, lifetime commitment to his service. The slave would express his desire to his master. In response, his master would use a sharp tool to pierce a permanent hole in the ear of his slave. That hole forever marked the man as a bond servant. His was not an eight-hour-a-day job. He was on call twenty-four hours a day. He did not have a contract; he had no guaranteed income or benefits. The bond servant was totally at the mercy of his master to provide adequately for his needs. His only concern as a bond servant was to be available and obedient.

Of course, this deep, lifetime commitment does not guarantee instant spiritual perfection. Our once-and-for-all surrender to God must be activated and appropriated daily. But it is the initial, total commitment that forms a basis for subsequent obedience.

Have you ever waved the white flag of surrender to the Lord Jesus? Are you building your life on the foundation of a nonnegotiable commitment to the Lordship of Christ and the authority of Scripture? If so, then every minute of your day, every dollar of your income, every ounce of your strength, mind, will, and emotions—all belong to Him. He makes all decisions. Our responsibility and privilege is merely to let Him use us to carry out His desires. A complete, lifetime surrender to Jesus allows His full, abundant, supernatural life to be released in us and sets us free from the power of temptation, sin, and self.

The hymn writer expressed it well when he wrote:

> I have decided to follow Jesus.
> No turning back.
>
> Though no one join me, still I will follow.
> No turning back.
>
> The world behind me, the cross before me.
> No turning back. No turning back.

Chapter 6

Whose Church Are We Building?

There is a great deal of talk about church growth these days. The mega-church has become a phenomenon of our time. Churches are bigger and better equipped than ever. We have more technology available to assist us in reaching the world than any previous generation. Despite all of this, we are not succeeding in making a significant impact on our society.

Perhaps our impotence is related to the fact that so many of us in the ministry are more interested in building up our name or that of our religious organization than we are in seeing the name of Christ lifted up.

The modern evangelical church is as guilty of ecclesiastical idolatry as any church hierarchy of the Middle Ages. Many of us are building our kingdoms rather than His kingdom. If we would spend as much time and effort promoting Jesus as we do promoting ourselves and our programs, we might be able to reach this world for Christ.

Further, the spirit and values of our age have infiltrated Christendom today to an alarming degree. Self-promotion has replaced self-denial, and self-indulgence has replaced self-control. We are not really all that different from the crowd Jesus rebuked in His time. They followed Him for all the wrong reasons. Many professing Christians do the same thing today. They are caught up in the bigness and excitement of the church, but they are not caught up in love with Jesus. They are willing to follow Him only if it costs them nothing.

Much of what is happening in today's church can be explained by hard work, marketing techniques, and borrowed money. God is not essential to our equation for success. Our Lord rebuked those who followed Him for the wrong reasons, but we are unwilling to do so because we have worked so hard to get a crowd that we are afraid to lose them. Instead of challenging their motives we want to soothe their consciences. No wonder the church has become a laughingstock in the secular world!

FAULTY MATERIALS

Bob had been a church music director and taught Bible in a Christian school in Des Moines, Iowa, for nearly ten years when God exposed to him the shallowness of his own ministry. "For nine years," he admitted to his students, "I've told you to pray and read the Bible. But I must confess that during this time, I have not prayed except in public, and I have not read the Bible except to prepare for a sermon or a lesson."

In his honesty and vulnerability, Bob told those students what they already knew. They sensed something was missing in his life. Their Bible lessons were dull and routine. But as he asked their forgiveness, they warmly embraced him and forgave him. Bob's humility began to produce a new zeal for God and His Word. A fresh enthusiasm gripped him as he plunged into the Scripture with a renewed hunger for God. Immediately that enthusiasm spilled over into the classroom, which became a laboratory instead of a lecture hall. Those young people began to experience God alive in their midst.

A pastor of a large church near Dallas, Texas, once told me that we have created a structure in our churches that will not allow for real spiritual growth. "If we took time to let God take over," he admitted, "our entire schedule and structure would be ruined." The tragedy is that if we do not let God take over, all else is ruined anyway.

The apostle Paul warned that "every man's work shall be made manifest: for the day shall declare it, because it shall be revealed by fire; and the fire shall try every man's work of what sort it is" (1 Cor. 3:13). In the same passage the apostle reminds us that Jesus Christ alone is the foundation of the church. His warning is that we take heed how we build on that foundation as well as what we build.

In fact, God is much more concerned *how* we build His church than *what* we build. Whenever the light of His glory goes out in the church, what do people emphasize? The fixtures! They talk about the organ, the choir loft, the kitchen, the fellowship hall, the stained-glass windows, and all the things that amount to nothing more than wood, hay, and stubble.

We hear a lot of glowing reports of church growth in America today. But I'm afraid that we may be experiencing more church swelling than real church growth. If I ram my head into a wall and my head gets bigger, it didn't grow! It just swelled!

Give me a few hours, and I could fill the largest church auditorium in North America. I could simply haul in tons of tumbleweed and fill the church. But you torch that building, and it all goes up in smoke in a matter of moments. The parallel is obvious—we have packed our churches with people who are lured by Madison Avenue-type promotion, hyped-up programs designed to cater to every special interest, and dazzling productions built around celebrities and showy music. But the increased attendance figures do not necessarily reflect church growth. In reality, we may have a case of church swelling!

On the other hand, to fill a building with precious metals that will withstand the test of fire is a task that cannot be accomplished in a few hours. That is the whole point of Paul's contrast between the gold, silver, and precious stones which cannot be mass-produced or manufactured by natural means, and the wood, hay, and stubble of human effort (see 1 Cor. 3:11–15). Gold, silver, and precious stones are not produced quickly or easily. They are only formed under intense pressure and over long periods of time.

In much the same way, it takes time to develop true disciples. Too many of us want to hurry up and get people converted, baptized, and plugged into the church program without taking time to properly or effectively disciple them. Qualities like obedience, morality, holiness, and purity are not the instantaneous results of some quick formula. All we do in the arm of the flesh will one day be torched and go up in smoke. But when the fires of persecution or judgment are applied, that which is truly the work of God will stand the test. In the refining fire, the precious metals survive—all else is destroyed.

This concept, properly understood, might radically alter our approach to ministry. When Elisha's servant failed to raise the Shunammite woman's son to life, the prophet himself went into the room and prayed and thrust himself upon the child until he came back to life (see 2 Kings 4:18–37).

Notice that Elisha "went into" the room with a sense of purpose and commitment. He "shut the door" as an act of devotion to God alone. He was not there to put on a show. Then "he prayed"—and, oh, how that prophet could pray! Then he laid his life on the child—eye to eye, mouth to mouth, hand to hand. This is the great failure of the modern church. We have gimmicks, gadgets, methods, and programs, but we do not have a life message to lay upon spiritually dead people that can result in true revival. Every component part of Elisha touched that boy until he came to life. The text also emphasizes that Elisha did not stop with a single effort, but he persisted with determination and perseverance until God raised the child.

The American church is powerless because we do not have enough preachers whose lives are pure and who are really living what they are preaching. Their messages are in their minds but not in their lives. They talk further than they walk, and, therefore, they cannot lead people into a powerful relationship with God.

In order to avoid facing the truth about ourselves, we emphasize the good in our lives and ministries and overlook that which is shallow or even evil. Revival will never come as long as we keep sweeping our sin under the rug of our own spiritual failure. Our *high* church doctrine often causes us to hold a *low* doctrine of Christ. We are afraid to let Him be Lord of our lives and churches because He might be more interested in examining the lives of our members than in hearing how many baptisms we've had this year.

DISCIPLE-MAKING AND THE GREAT COMMISSION

One of our problems is that we no longer possess a clear sense of the God-ordained nature and mission of the church. As you attend church services from week to week, do you ever ask yourself, "Why does the church exist and what is its purpose?"

We will only succeed in accomplishing our purpose if we know what that purpose is. The church's supreme purpose is to glorify God, but how does the church glorify God? I believe that Jesus' final instructions to His followers before He ascended into heaven provide a key to understanding how the church is to glorify God.

Jesus said, "All authority in heaven and on earth has been given to Me. Therefore go and make disciples of all nations, baptizing them in the name of the Father and of the Son and of the Holy Spirit, and teaching them to obey everything I have commanded you" (Matt. 28:18–20 NIV).

Jesus was leaving the earth, but He passed on to His followers His God-given authority. For what purpose? That they might carry on the work He began—the process of disciple-making.

DISCIPLE-MAKING is a twofold **process** which involves both **evangelism** (spiritual birth) and **edification** (spiritual growth).

PROCESS:	Evangelism (Birth)	+	Edification (Growth)
PRODUCT:	Spiritual Maturity (Col. 1:28) Christ-likeness (Gal. 4:19) Committed Reproducers (2 Tim. 2:2)		

Too often we try to separate these two phases of the disciple-making process. Some ministries, individuals, and churches place all of their emphasis on building up the saints, but have lost a vision for the evangelism of the lost. It is impossible to be spiritually mature and not share God's burden for those who are without Christ. One sign of physical health and maturity is the capacity to reproduce. So it is in the spiritual realm   As the early church built itself up, the believers were constantly being used by the Spirit to win new converts to Christ. The church stayed dynamic and fresh as long as there was this ongoing cycle of spiritual birth and growth.

On the other hand, many ministries, churches, and individuals are engaged in evangelism to the exclusion of edification (building a believer to spiritual maturity). The result is that those churches are full of spiritual babies. The writer of the book of Hebrews appealed to his readers to leave the baby doctrines, to grow up spiritually, and to press on to maturity. He reminded them that in light of the time they had known Christ, "Ye ought to be teachers" (Heb. 5:12; 6:1). Instead, they were still dependent on someone to teach them the basic truths of the Christian life.

In the parable of the sower, Jesus illustrated the results of bringing people to Christ, but neglecting their further spiritual growth in Christ. "Some [seed] fell upon stony places, where they had not much earth: and forthwith they sprung up, because they had no deepness of earth: And when the sun was up, they were scorched; and because they had no root, they withered away" (Matt. 13:5,6).

When we look at the salvation statistics of many of our churches, we must ask ourselves some tough questions: Where are those new converts? Are they going on with Christ? Are they learning to feed themselves spiritually? Are they leading others to Christ and building them to maturity? Or are they merely occupying pews in the church building? Worse, have they fallen away altogether?

It is a crime to bring a physical baby into the world and refuse to care for it. The privilege of giving birth cannot be separated from the responsibility to feed, clothe, protect, and care for that child until he is old enough to care for himself. As Christians, we have an equally great responsibility to nurture our children in the faith.

PRODUCT OF DISCIPLE-MAKING

We have seen that disciple-making is a process involving both evangelism and edification. But what is the desired end product of disciple-making? Paul expressed the desire that his converts would be "perfect [mature] in Christ" (Col. 1:28). He referred to the Galatian believers as "my little children, of whom I travail in birth again until Christ be formed in you" (Gal. 4:19). God's goal for every believer is that we become spiritually mature, perfectly conformed to the image of Christ (Rom. 8:29). This means that every aspect of the believer's life (his motives, responses, and attitudes) will be like Jesus. This then must be our goal for ourselves and for each other.

Let me express it another way. The product of disciple-making is committed reproducers. "Committed" describes what a disciple *is*. "Reproducer" describes what a disciple *does*.

The New Testament illustrates at least three distinct levels of commitment a disciple may have. In Jesus' day there were thousands of *professing* disciples. These followed Jesus because they were intrigued by His miracles. But when Jesus began to lay down the requirements of true discipleship, many of these disciples deserted

Him. They had no genuine, lasting commitment to Christ (John 2:23–25; 6:64,66).

Then there were *possessing* disciples (John 2:11). These genuinely believed that Jesus was who He said He was. But Jesus called these disciples to a still deeper level of commitment. He wanted them to become *progressing* disciples. This is the commitment to which Jesus calls each of us. There are at least eight characteristics of a progressing disciple. Which ones are true of your life?

(1) *Christ-centered love.* Our love for Jesus is to be so intense and fervent that all other loves seem, by comparison, to be as hatred (Luke 14:26). Such love for Jesus is characterized by obedience to His commandments (John 14:15–24) and deep devotion (Phil. 3:7–14).

(2) *Compassion for the brethren.* Jesus said that our love for each other would convince the watching world that we are His disciples (John 13:35). The apostle John repeats this truth over and over again in his first epistle. It is impossible, he says, to be a true disciple, and not love your brother. It is impossible to love God and not love the other members of His family.

(3) *Continual self-denial.* "If any man will come after me, let him deny himself . . ." (Matt. 16:24). Like Jesus, the progressing disciple does not claim any rights of his own, but completely yields himself to God (Rom. 6:13).

(4) *Choosing the cross.* ". . . let him . . . take up his cross . . ." (Matt. 16:24). Christ's disciples are to expect (and even anticipate and glory in) suffering (1 Peter 4:12; 2 Tim. 3:12).

(5) *Chasing after Christ.* ". . . and follow me" (Matt. 16:24). Following Christ is a way of life which requires careful consideration and personal sacrifice. Jesus discouraged people from following Him without first counting the cost.

(6)   *Continuing in the Word.* Spiritual sustenance, direction, and life are found as we abide in His Word and allow His Word to abide in us (John 15:7; Col. 3:16).

(7)   *Casting all on Christ.* Jesus insisted that His disciples be willing to forsake all (possessions, prestige, popularity, prosperity) in order to follow Him (Luke 14:33).

(8)   *Consistent prayer life.* Jesus taught His disciples that commitment to prayer was essential if they were to have victory over the weakness of their flesh (Matt. 26:41).

The goal of disciple-making is to develop progressing disciples. However, it is not enough that Christ's disciples be personally committed. They are also to be reproducers. In the physical realm, a baby is cared for, grows up, becomes an adult, marries, and reproduces. Apart from this ongoing cycle of growth and reproduction, eventually there would be no human race!

In the spiritual realm, we are also expected to multiply and be reproducers. Jesus was the model reproducer. Mark 3:14 tells us that He chose twelve men, "that they should be with Him, and that He might send them forth . . . ." Jesus invested three years training these twelve men to follow Him, teaching them how to have a right relationship with God and how to win converts, build them in the faith, and send them out to win, build, and send others. After Jesus left the earth, it was those few men He had trained who multiplied and reproduced the life of Christ in others. In just a few years, the whole known world had been evangelized by the products of that disciple-making ministry (Acts 17:6).

INSECURITY AND THE FEAR OF MAN

When true revival comes, it restores the church to true New Testament Christianity. Such revival focuses our attention on God and not on ourselves. One of the great reasons for failure in the disciple-making process is our own insecurity and fear of people. Some of us are so insecure that we are afraid to let God have control of our lives, our families, and our churches. Too many pastors are doing little more than buttering up the deacons, blasting the people, and manipulating the results. They are seeking to control everything in the church out of fear of man, rather than being driven and motivated by the fear of the Lord.

The Bible warns us: "The fear of man bringeth a snare: but whoso putteth his trust in the LORD shall be safe" (Prov. 29:25). The fear of man imprisons our souls and leaves us in bondage to our own insecurity. The fear of man has immobilized far too many of God's people and held them captive to the expectations of others.

Several years ago, God began to deal with me about insecurity and the fear of man in my own life. I was a successful evangelist by outward appearances, but I often found myself struggling in this area of my life. Insecurity is the result of placing trust or confidence in people or things that can be taken away from you. When we put our trust in such things, we are not free to trust God fully.

Everything earthly is temporal and can be taken away from us: mate, ministry, health, sanity, intellect, personality, friends, abilities, finances, and material prosperity. Unfortunately, most of us have built our lives on these very things. When our health fails, when people disappoint us, when our finances are depleted, we despair because we trusted those things for our security.

One of the evidences of insecurity in religious circles is the degree to which we use fear, force, and intimidation to accomplish our objectives. So much of what results can be explained apart from the power of God.

Insecurity and fear of other people account for the reason many preachers find themselves unable or unwilling to preach what they know to be true, because they feel threatened by the movement or association in which they find themselves. Their mistake is that they trust in human leaders and not in God Himself. Driven by the need for the approval of others, they cannot stand up for what they know is right.

By contrast, security is the result of placing our confidence and trust in that which cannot be taken away from us. It causes us to focus on the spiritual, not the material, and on the eternal, not the temporal. Security comes when our ultimate confidence is in Jesus Christ and His eternal Word of truth.

At the time God began dealing with me about this matter of insecurity, I heard a godly pastor speak on the "fear of man" (which is the biblical term for insecurity). As he preached, God confronted my pride in a deep, dramatic way. I realized that much of my life and ministry was rooted in the fear of man, and that I needed God to remove it from my life.

I recall pastors telling me over the years that they were afraid to have our ministry in their churches because of what someone else might think of them. Others would tell me not to preach in certain places because of what some Christian leader might say about me. I finally began to see that all of this was nothing more than idolatry—ecclesiastical idolatry. Men were putting the opinions and approval of others above that of God.

Insecure preachers are constantly threatened and intimidated by what others think about them. Therefore, they keep everyone at a distance. They portray the tough-guy image and try to keep everybody else on a guilt trip. That is why so many in the ministry are so driven to be in control of everything. Controllers are insecure by their very nature. They fear being compared with anyone—even their own staff members. Many have never been delivered from the ecclesiastical games preachers play. Their looks, dress, talk, and terminology all reveal their human loyalties but say little about their loyalty to God.

Preachers are often afraid of true revival because they fear it will expose them or their ministries for what they really are. They want their people to get right with God, but most of them do not intend to let God really get hold of them. They are too worried about maintaining their image, status, numbers, statistics, income, and lifestyle.

In my own pilgrimage on this matter, I had to face the fact that I had filled my life with activity and busyness to appear successful and thereby gain the approval of others. I realized how self-centered and self-serving such an attitude was. I also realized that God said He was well pleased with His Son whom He approved. Then it hit me! The approval of God is what I ought to be seeking, not the approval of other people.

I remember as a young preacher feeling consumed with what others thought of my preaching. At the close of a service, I was on edge until I knew that the pastor, deacons, and everybody else liked my message! When God began to change my heart, I found myself leaving the platform, going to my knees before I had talked with anyone else, and asking, "Lord, was that all right with You? Were You pleased? Because if You are pleased with me, that's all that matters."

Whenever we substitute other things for God's approval, we will end up ensnared in the fear of man. Substitutes for God's approval may include:

(1) *Acceptance.* Some of us want to be accepted so badly we will do anything to pacify people so they will like us. This drive to be accepted may keep us from confronting others in relation to the needs in their lives.

(2) *Status.* Others are driven by the pride of position or possessions. They have to maintain a certain status at all costs. The clothes they wear, the house they live in, the car they drive, the salary they command, the size church they pastor—these can become all-important matters to an insecure man who is seeking to find approval through status.

(3)   *Productivity.*   Still others seek approval through performance.   They believe they must constantly remain busy in order to prove their worth.

For years, I was so caught up in this last point that in the early days of my ministry, pastors often rebuked me for neglecting them. I ran into one pastor who reminded me, "Del, when you were with us ten years ago, I never saw you except in the services. You were on six different flights out of town that week. You ran all over the country, and when you were in town, you ran all over town!"

I realized that I was caught up in seeking approval through productivity and performance.   I thought people would think better of me because I was so busy. I never took vacations. I did not dare to relax. I just kept going day and night—for all the wrong reasons. What an incredible release and freedom it was for me to begin to seek only to be approved unto God.

I'll never forget hearing a pastor stand before his people during a crusade and transparently listing for them the specific symptoms of insecurity and fear of man in his life.

- Defensiveness—feeling the need to tell my side of the story to people who aren't involved.

- Jealousy—fear that others will be liked for their teaching more than I am for mine.

- Overeating—to cover up and compensate for my insecurities.

- Anger—at those who criticize me.

- Resentment—for being misunderstood and not being adequately appreciated.

- Insensitivity—to others who are hurting.

- Fear—of my ministry failing.

- Depression—over not feeling worthy or loved.

- Inability to be tender with my wife—can't share my heart; can't say "I love you" or "I need you."

- Can't sit down and talk openly with my children or my parents.

- Can't express need—have to leave the impression that I have everything under control, and that I can handle anything that comes along.

This pastor went on to share how he had discovered that his insecurity was rooted in pride and self-focus. Humility coupled with developing a holy and healthy fear of God resulted in his being set free from the bondage of the fear of man.

I remember a CPA in one of our crusades who was convicted by God that he had misappropriated money in his corporation. When he confessed this to his company, he lost his job and all the security that went with it. When I asked him if it was worth all that to have a pure heart and a clear conscience, he replied, "Absolutely. I was really just more concerned about my reputation than I was about God's reputation."

Some time after God began to deal with me about the issue of insecurity and the fear of man, my staff scheduled me to preach in a setting where I knew a particular Christian leader would be in the audience. God had used this man's ministry in a powerful way in my life, and I held him in the highest esteem. Knowing his grasp of biblical truth, I kept wondering what he would think of my message. Finally, God questioned me: "Whose church are you building—Mine or yours? Whom are you trying to impress—Me or that man?"

Moments before I was to speak, I was still struggling with that hideous insecurity. One of my staff handed me a note that said, "Del, this is your 'final exam' in 'The Fear of Man'!" Immediately, I saw my feelings for what they were and was able to thank God for this opportunity to seek His approval, regardless of what anyone else thought.

The constant realization that it is *His* church, not ours, *His* kingdom, not ours, and that our calling is not to be a success, but to be faithful, will set us free from that man-fearing, people-pleasing spirit.

Chapter 7

Why Are We Drifting With the Culture?

Bonnie was typical of many of today's Christians. She was married and had two children and a fabulous job. The only problem was that her job was ruining her marriage. It kept her from her husband and children and kept all of them from church.

"Oh, we came occasionally," Bonnie told me, "but I let fear, pride, and a general lack of faith keep me from doing what I really needed to do in my life. I was so in love with my job that I couldn't be in love with God, let alone my husband and children."

Like many of today's materialistic Christians, Bonnie worked hard to have it all—house, cars, clothes, and status. But she slowly drifted away from God and her family. "I let all those things become idols in my life," she confessed. But when God turned her life around, He turned it all the way around.

"I had to learn to trust God all over again," she said. "I had put my trust in my job and the things it provided for me. That was when God let me know that idol had to go if I was ever going to know God's blessing in my life or family again."

The modern church has made an idol of materialism and has bowed to it for so long she is oblivious to her own condition. Churches are so busy imitating the world that they cannot change the world. The favorite invitation appeal of today's church seems to be, "Accept Christ and go on our ski trip."

In a nation where the church is exploding statistically, we should expect it to be having an incredible impact spiritually. But that is not the case! Adultery, divorce, bitterness, rebellion, anxiety, and spiritual emptiness are as prevalent in the church as they are outside it. We are not significantly changing the culture because we are drifting with the culture.

Identifying and renouncing our idols is the only way to stop the church's capitulation to the sinful culture which threatens to engulf it.

GOLDEN CALVES

Moses must have been shocked. Surely he was just having a bad dream. But the sights and sounds that greeted him as he descended from the mountain were real. The noise was deafening. Cacophonous music had reached a feverish pitch. The camp was in a state of utter chaos. Discarded pieces of clothing were strewn everywhere, and as far as the eye could see, a mass of human flesh gyrated to the rhythm of the music.

Only six weeks earlier he had left behind a well-ordered, spiritually sensitive congregation. Why then this frenzied, lewd orgy? Fierce anger and hurt welled up within Moses' breast as his eyes moved to the object that occupied the center of attention. There stood a crude, roughly-fashioned likeness of a calf. It reminded him of figures he had seen in Egypt. Moses' presence seemed to go unnoticed until, with a sudden, swift motion, he dashed to the ground the stone tablets which he had just received from God. They now lay broken beyond repair. When he did so, the party came to a screeching halt. All eyes turned to see what would happen next.

The pieces of rock that lay at Moses' feet summed up what had happened. God revealed Himself and gave His law to His chosen people. At the core of that revelation was the requirement that Jehovah God alone was to be worshiped. God strictly prohibited the forming or worshiping of any images or likenesses of pagan deities. In breaking the first and greatest commandment, this newly formed congregation was guilty of breaking the whole law.

The New Testament commentary on this incident indicates that it was recorded in Scripture as an example, "for our admonition." The admonition Paul gives is twofold: "Let him that thinketh he standeth take heed lest he fall," and "Flee from idolatry" (1 Cor. 10:12,14). What is Paul saying? Simply that the church today can fall into idolatry as easily as that church in the wilderness did, and that we must aggressively, actively guard ourselves against every form of idolatry.

Israel's experience with the golden calf provides some valuable insights for twentieth-century worshipers.

Believers can succumb to idolatry.

The idolaters of Exodus 32 were not pagans but were a people who had already been redeemed. The Israelites had recently witnessed the supernatural power of God at the Red Sea, they had received God's Word in the form of the Ten Commandments, and they had made a firm commitment to obey God and His Word (Ex. 19:8; 24:3). The word "idolatry" today conjures up mental images of unreached tribes on the other side of the globe. But this story indicates that no one is exempt from the temptation of idolatry—even blood-bought believers who know God's Word and have made a commitment to Him can fall into this heinous sin.

Impatience leads to sin.

Moses left the people at the foot of Mount Sinai while he went up the mountain to meet with God and receive directions for the tabernacle worship. The people had explicit instructions to wait for Moses to return. However, they grew tired of waiting, "And when the people saw that

Moses delayed to come down out of the mount, the people gathered themselves together unto Aaron, and said unto him, Up, make us gods . . ." (Ex. 32:1). In the face of delayed gratification, rather than waiting for God to act, the people erected an idol to satisfy the demands of their flesh. How like our instant-everything generation which lives for the here and now and knows so little about waiting on God. Every craving must be satisfied immediately and visibly.

Spiritual leaders can become a party to idolatry.

Notice that the Israelites sinned with the full knowledge and participation of their spiritual leaders. Aaron and Hur had spiritual responsibility for the people in Moses' absence. No mention is made of Hur in the golden calf incident. Perhaps he preferred not to buck the tide. Regardless, we know that Aaron lacked the character, conviction, courage, and commitment to resist the people's pleas. Not only did he allow them to construct an idol, he actually gave direction to the project. The problem was that Aaron, unlike Moses, had not ever really come face-to-face with God. He had heard about God from Moses, but he didn't know God personally. As a result, he was not able to withstand temptation or confront the people over their wrongdoing.

People can give sacrificially to a wrong cause.

We see next that the people gave sacrificially to construct the golden calf. There was no reluctance to sacrifice their most prized jewels for something that brought temporary pleasure.

Today we find that many believers readily spend large sums of money, are willing to be inconvenienced, and make enormous sacrifices to fulfill the lusts of their flesh. On the other hand, many part with only useless, missionary barrel rejects for the cause of Christ, and that only in response to repeated, fervent, emotional appeals.

Idolatry appeals to the desires of the flesh.

Exodus 32:4 illustrates the fleshly drive to worship that which is visible, tangible, and temporal. How ludicrous, we think, that the

Israelites, who had a covenant relationship with Jehovah, would prostrate and prostitute themselves before a lifeless, impotent, melted-down collection of earrings! Yet, was their idolatry really much different than that of many believers today whose gods of temporal, fleshly values demand their devotion, focus, and commitment?

Idolatry can be mixed with true worship.

We also see in this passage the tendency to mix worship of idols with worship of the true and living God. When the calf was completed, Aaron "built an altar before it, and . . . made proclamation, and said, Tomorrow is a feast to the LORD. And they rose up early on the morrow, and offered burnt offerings, and brought peace offerings" (Ex. 32:5,6). As if it weren't wicked enough to forsake God and worship a false god, the people blasphemed and degraded the name of Jehovah by professing to worship Him while bowing down before the altar of the golden calf.

The tragedy is that even while speaking and singing the praises of Jehovah in our churches, we may at the same time be bowing our hearts and wills before the false gods of our age. Our deceitful hearts may say, "We are worshiping God," but God knows better.

Idolatry turns us away from the true God.

The worship of the golden calf caused the Israelites to forget the true God and what He had done for them. They attributed their successes and victories to the work of their own hands rather than to the God who had made them, and they said, "These be thy gods, O Israel, which brought thee up out of the land of Egypt" (v. 4).

And so it is today that we so easily forget the source of our blessings and strengths and begin mistakenly, proudly to credit our own efforts with making our successes and achievements possible.

Idolatry and immorality go hand in hand.

The worship of the golden calf was closely associated with the pursuit of sensual fulfillment. "The people sat down to eat and to drink, and rose up to play" (v. 6). Raucous music, dancing, perversion, and immodesty accompanied the worship of the golden calf. Things are really no different with our hedonistic, pleasure-seeking generation which is bent on self-gratification. How the heart of God must be grieved as He beholds His people offering pious lip service to Him on the one hand, while on the other hand indulging our flesh and promoting every conceivable form of worldliness and sensuality.

Idolatry causes us to turn back to the world.

The New Testament gives additional insight into the root cause of Israel's lapse into idolatry. In their hearts they turned back again into Egypt (Acts 7:39). Here is the real source of all idol worship by the people of God. It is a matter of the heart. This was not just an innocent, accidental slip-up by the Israelites. They deliberately willed to transfer the focus, attention, and affection of their hearts from Jehovah back to Egypt, from whence they had been redeemed. Forgotten were the 430 years of bondage, cruelty, and tears they endured in that land. They were willing to forfeit the promises of God—the blessings, the land, the future, a heritage—on the altar of a god that they could see and touch and from which they could derive momentary satisfaction.

The lapse into idolatry can come in an instant.

Notice that the Israelites did not drift into idolatry over a period of time. The Scripture makes it clear that they "turned aside quickly" (Ex. 32:8) out of the worship of God.

As surely as He did then, Jehovah God sees the spiritual idolatry of His people today. He knows the true condition of our hearts. He knows what we love. He knows what is really important to us.

The writer of the book of Hebrews reminds us that it takes less than twenty-four hours for our hearts to turn back to other gods, to be "hardened through the deceitfulness of sin" (Heb. 3:13).

True, we have not erected golden calves in our churches and homes, but what about other idols that have usurped His rightful place as Lord of our lives and God of His church?

There are two characteristics that idols have in common. God said to Moses, "They have made them a molten calf, and have worshiped it, and have sacrificed thereunto . . ." (Ex. 32:8). An idol may be said to be any person or thing (1) which is the object of our focus, attention, affection, or worship or (2) for which we are willing to make sacrifices.

OTHER IDOLS

What are some of the gods which have stolen the hearts of twentieth-century believers? In Paul's letters to Timothy, he warned about several gods that could easily become the object of our love and compete with God for His place as the supreme object of our devotion and sacrifice.

Love of Self (2 Tim. 3:2)
This god takes many forms. It is at the heart of our preoccupation with the body, physical beauty, and glamour. It reveals itself in our insistence that we have a right to be happy, even if that means divorcing a mate or pursuing a career and leaving children at home to fend for themselves. It is love of self that causes us to cling to "my rights," "my time," "my privacy," "my career," "my reputation," "my future," and on and on.

It is love of self that causes us to want everybody and everything to revolve around us, and that considers every decision in the light of "what is best for me."

Love of self causes us to protect and defend ourselves when our needs are pointed out, and to refuse to admit to God or anyone else that we are not all that we have appeared to be.

Love of self is at the root of stubbornness (which is "as the sin of . . . idolatry"—1 Sam. 15:23)—exalting "my way" above all others.

Moral impurity is one of the supreme manifestations of this insatiable love of self. Self-gratification, self-centeredness, self-sufficiency—all these are merely different faces of the god of self.

101

Love of Pleasure (2 Tim. 3:4)

We are a pleasure-crazed generation. There seems to be no limit to the sacrifices we will make for the god of pleasure. We are driven in mad pursuit of pleasures—vacations, television shows, VCRs, fine dining, sports events, entertainment, hobbies, sensual pleasures, magazines, books, music—anything to titillate our senses and make us feel good. This god is never satisfied. Every time it is fed, it craves more.

This idol has even found a home in Christendom. Often the church that draws the biggest crowd is the church with the most dynamic entertainment, a star-studded lineup of celebrity speakers, the most expensive sports complexes, the most comfortable pews, carpet, and air conditioning, and the most alluring schedule of activities for every member of the family—aerobics classes, square dancing, quilting parties, roller skating parties, bowling and softball leagues, and of course, lots of church dinners and picnics.

Whatever happened to taking up our cross and following Christ? Whatever happened to preaching and programs that discipline the flesh and build the spirit? The god of pleasure has even wooed us with the pleasures of sin. Forgetting that the pleasures of sin are but for a moment, we have tolerated and winked at every possible expression of sensuality and promiscuity, even among professing Christians. Fornication, adultery, incest, and pornographic magazines, books, and movies have become commonplace in God's temple.

In the process of pampering our flesh and indulging our lusts and desires, we have lost sight of the purpose for which we exist: "For Thou hast created all things, and for Thy pleasure they . . . were created" (Rev. 4:11). Our primary purpose in life is not to be happy. Our primary purpose in life is to be holy and to bring pleasure to the heart of God. Furthermore, genuine, lasting pleasure is not to be found in any created thing, but only in the presence of God: "In Thy presence is fulness of joy; at Thy right hand there are pleasures for evermore" (Ps. 16:11).

Love of Money (1 Tim. 6:10)

Perhaps no idol has done more to sap believers of spiritual vitality and to diminish our capacity to respond to God than has the god of money. For many of us, our philosophy of life may be summarized by the bumper sticker which reads: "He who dies with the most toys—wins." The acquisition of things and material prosperity occupies our time, our efforts, our focus. It's not that having those things is necessarily wrong, but we have set our sights on the things money can buy, at the expense of those eternal riches money can never buy.

The problem is not in having nice things, but in loving, seeking, and intensely desiring them. It's a matter of priorities. Our goals and checkbooks reveal what is really important to us. Most of us are consumed with buying, spending, and saving for things that will be worthless in eternity. Our obsession with houses, cars, clothes, fashions, sports equipment, recreational vehicles, stocks, bonds, and investments has strangled the life of Christ right out of our hearts. We have planned for retirement, but we have not prepared for the return of Christ. Our plans, goals, and ambitions center around that which is seen, while we give little, if any, thought and effort to leaving a heritage of godliness and righteousness to our children.

Those who crave the wealth of this world must count the cost that will be required. "But they that will be rich fall into temptation and a snare, and into many foolish and hurtful lusts, which drown men in destruction and perdition" (1 Tim. 6:9). None of us, no matter how spiritually mature or committed, ever arrives at the point where we do not have to diligently guard against the love of money. Jesus' words need to be engrafted into our every conscious thought and waking moment: "Take heed, and beware of covetousness: for a man's life consisteth not in the abundance of the things which he possesseth" (Luke 12:15).

Love of This Present World (2 Tim. 4:10)

Those who worship this god live for the here and now and seldom take thought for the world to come. This god exalts personal comfort and convenience over the will of God. Those who are in love with the age in which we live are too soft and lazy to pick up a cross and develop Christ-like character. They are enamored with the philosophy of this age, and with the power, prestige, and popularity it has to offer. However, they are spiritually shortsighted and fail to see that this world and all that is in it is rapidly passing away. Those who cling to the enticements of this world will find themselves empty-handed on the other side of eternity.

OVERCOMING IDOLATRY

Idol worship always has a high price tag. The children of Israel did not consider the consequences of their choice to worship the golden calf. Their idolatry provoked the wrath of God, and 3,000 men paid for their sin with their lives. God had promised the Israelites His provision and His power, but now He said they would have to go on without His presence.

Loving anything or anyone more than God takes a toll on our physical, emotional, and spiritual well-being. The seeds of idolatry and temporal values are multiplied in a harvest of discontent, depression, and disillusionment. The love of self, pleasure, money, or this present world weakens the spirit and leaves us at the mercy of our physical lusts and appetites. Like thorns, cares and riches and pleasures of this life choke out the Word, and it brings no fruit to perfection in our lives.

That which we love and worship controls us. That is why Jesus said we cannot at the same time love both God and money or any other temporal thing. Our love, attention, devotion, and focus will be attached supremely to God and His righteousness or to the things of this world. We cannot love both. "Whosoever . . . will be a friend of the world is the enemy of God" (James 4:4). The love of the things of this world will surely erode our love for Jesus.

Is it any wonder then that the New Testament writers spoke such strong words of warning against idolatry? "Wherefore, my dearly beloved, flee from idolatry" (1 Cor. 10:14). "Little children, keep yourselves from idols" (1 John 5:21).

Repent and turn from every idol.

The golden calf incident illustrates two contrasting responses we may have when faced with our idolatry. Aaron's response, when confronted with his sin, was essentially one of indifference (Ex. 32:22). In effect, he said, "It's no big deal—nothing to get excited about." Then, in an effort to save his own neck, he blamed the people (v. 23) and lied to escape the reality of his failure (v. 24). Aaron, like many of us, would do anything but admit that he had sinned.

On the other hand, Moses responded to the situation with intense anger, accompanied by swift, decisive action. "He took the calf . . . and burnt it in the fire, and ground it to powder, and strawed it upon the water, and made the children of Israel drink of it" (Ex. 32:20).

There was no delaying, no deliberating, no hesitating, no attempt to salvage the valuable jewels which had been used to build the calf. The idol must be torn down; it must be utterly destroyed; every particle of it must be removed immediately. Oh, that God would give us the heart of this man of God, a holy hatred for all that would rival His place as Lord of our lives. Those who would be worshipers of God may not tolerate so much as a hint of love for that which is temporal.

Restore God to His rightful place.

Removing the idols in our lives leaves only empty pedestals behind. God must be restored to His rightful place as the one and only focus of our worship and devotion. All allegiance to things of this world must be transferred to the true and living God. We must consciously and deliberately set our hearts on Him.

The words of the hymn writer express the deep heart desire of every true child of God:

> The dearest idol I have known,
> Whate'er that idol be,
> Help me to tear it from Thy throne,
> And worship only Thee.

Young William Borden once set out to make his fortune. Upon graduation from high school, his businessman father sent young William on a cruise around the world. Brokenhearted by the spiritual needs of the people he met, William committed his life to serve Jesus Christ as a missionary.

He wrote in his journal,

> Say "no" to self, "yes" to Jesus every time. . . . In every man's heart there is a throne and a cross. If Christ is on the throne, self is on the cross; and if self, even a little bit, is on the throne, Jesus is on the cross in that man's heart . . . . Lord, I take my hands off, as far as my life is concerned. I put Thee on the throne of my life. Change, cleanse, use me as Thou shalt choose.

He dedicated his college years to mastering the Word of God and reaching those around him with the gospel of Christ. Throughout those years of preparation, William never wavered from the goal on which he had fixed his sight, although as an heir of the Borden Milk Company, he might have settled for a life of convenience and ease.

Finally, the time came for William to leave for the mission field. Headed for China, he sailed first to Egypt, where he contracted spinal meningitis and died less than a month later. Some would say, "What a waste."

But the seed of that solitary life, which went into the ground and died, has produced an abundant harvest of righteousness. Countless young men, inspired by his wholehearted devotion to Christ, have risen to take his place on the mission fields of the world.

When William's will was probated, it was discovered that he had left his entire fortune of over one million dollars to be invested in the cause of Christ, in addition to the thousands of dollars he had given away during his short lifetime.

It has been said that three phrases summarize William Borden's life:

No reserves.

No retreat.

No regrets.

May I ask you some personal questions: What are you living for? Is it worth dying for? Will you be able one day in heaven to face the Lord Jesus, who gave everything for you, and say, "No regrets"?

My friend, time is short, eternity is long, and Jesus is coming. When you stand before Him, and all that is earthly and temporal has vanished away, what riches of eternal value will you have to cast at His feet?

Can Dry Bones Live Again?

Part Three

Chapter 8

It Has Happened Before

It is never too late for God to send revival and reverse His judgment until that judgment is final. Even when the nation of Israel faced God's ultimate judgment through impending invasion, war, and captivity, God still looked for a man to stand in the gap (Ezek. 22:30). In His compassion, God did not want to send judgment. All He wanted was one man to be willing to make a difference.

Later, in his prophecy of the dry bones (ch. 37), the prophet Ezekiel predicted that God would yet send revival to His people. Ezekiel was taken in the spirit to a desert valley filled with dry bones that had been scattered about. "These bones are the whole house of Israel," God told the prophet (v. 11). Then the Lord promised to send His Spirit into them that they might live and be restored to their land (v. 14). Then Ezekiel prophesied and the bones came together; the Spirit of God empowered them, and they came back to life.

Revival is a supernatural action that comes sovereignly from the hand of God. Revival is the Reviver Himself in action in the inner life of His church. No one can bring revival or manufacture its results. We can pray for it, weep for it, repent of our sins, and wait upon God to move, but we cannot make revival happen.

Human efforts brought about by advertising and promotional schemes, electronically-enhanced music, computerized visitation lists, and just plain hard work will not in themselves bring revival. All of that may be good in its place, but that is not sufficient to bring a visitation of God upon His church.

Genuine revival is the extraordinary movement of the Holy Spirit upon our lives. It results in a deep conviction of sin and a deeper work of spiritual cleansing in our lives. When revival comes, God's glory is manifest and His presence is evident. The whole church becomes ablaze with His glory!

Revival restores our first love for Christ. It resets our focus upon Him alone. It redirects our energies to serve Him alone. It reorganizes our priorities to obey Him alone. Genuine revival brings back the glory of God that has often departed from our lives. It restores the joy in our relationship to God and to one another.

Revival also resolves conflict in the church. When our hearts are broken before God, His love flows out of us to everybody around us. The surest sign that a church needs revival is when jealousy and conflict prevail. Revival changes all of that because it removes bitterness, renews the mind, refreshes the spirit, and redirects the energies of our lives to serve God.

LORD, DO IT AGAIN

Some time ago, someone handed me a copy of the front page of the *Denver Post*. The date was January 20, 1905. The headlines across the top of the page read:

Entire city pauses for prayer at the high tide of business as the soul rises above sordid thoughts—remarkable outburst of gospel sentiment provoked by revival—Evangelist Chapman and his associates cause a hush to spread over the population, while the noonday meetings draw congregations unprecedented in numbers.

The opening paragraphs of the lengthy article described the noonday prayer meetings that took place in the early weeks of 1905 as revival swept the city of Denver.

> For two hours at midday all Denver was held in a spell. . . . The marts of trade were deserted between noon and two o'clock this afternoon, and all worldly affairs were forgotten, and the entire city was given over to meditation of higher things. The Spirit of the Almighty pervaded every nook. Going to and coming from the great meetings, the thousands of men and women radiated this Spirit which filled them, and the clear Colorado sunshine was made brighter by the reflected glow of the light of God shining from happy faces. Seldom has such a remarkable sight been witnessed—an entire great city, in the middle of a busy week day, bowing before the throne of heaven and asking and receiving the blessing of the King of the Universe.

Apparently, it was the memory of a similar outpouring of God's Spirit that prompted the psalmist to pen the words of Psalm 85. In the first three verses, he prays in essence, "Lord, You've done it before . . . ." He reflects on the freedom (v. 1), forgiveness (v. 2), and restored fellowship (v. 3) that God had brought to His people in times past.

The memory of past manifestations of the power of God motivates us to seek Him for a fresh moving in our midst. And so the psalmist cries out in verses 4–7, "Lord, do it again!" This is the heartcry of a man who is not satisfied with a ho-hum, explainable, subnormal brand of Christianity. He speaks for those of us who long to see the fullest possible expression of the power and purity of God unleashed in His people.

The psalmist cried: "Wilt Thou not revive us again: that Thy people may rejoice in Thee?" (v. 6). Notice that it is God's people, not the lost, who are in need of revival. To revive means to bring back to life. The lost have never had spiritual life and need to be regenerated. Before the church can effectively reach a lost and needy world, we must first be revived, purified, emptied of sin and self, and filled with His Holy Spirit. In our unrevived state, we have nothing that would cause lost sinners to be drawn to Jesus.

God's Word reminds us that "judgment must begin at the house of God" (1 Peter 4:17). In the Old Testament, when God gave Ezekiel a vision of forthcoming judgment for sin, He instructed that the judgment was to "begin at My sanctuary" (Ezek. 9:6).

Not only is revival for God's people in general, but more specifically, I must acknowledge my personal need for revival. As the old spiritual puts it, "It's not my brother or my sister, / but it's me, Oh Lord, / standin' in the need of prayer." We tend to be acutely aware of the shortcomings and needs in the lives of everyone around us and yet are so easily blinded to our own needs. While God may graciously send revival to a number of believers in a given area, revival is not a spectator sport. It is intensely personal. Someone has wisely observed: "Revival is God's finger pointed at me!"

In our crusades, we ask people to fill out prayer cards so that our team can pray specifically for their burdens and needs. Invariably, during the first several days of the crusade, people will ask us to pray for their husband or wife, their wayward son or daughter, their backslidden friends, or their deacons or church staff to experience revival. But when the Spirit of God begins to break through, those cards begin to read more like this: "I thought my mate needed revival—but God has shown me that I am the one in need of revival." When we start to see our own needs, then we may believe that God will soon come and meet with us in genuine revival!

The nature of true revival may best be seen in the results that it brings about in the lives of God's people.

Revival brings a new love for God.

Revival brings, first, a new love for God. When asked by a Jewish legal expert which was the greatest of all the commandments, Jesus replied without hesitation, "Thou shalt love the Lord thy God with all thy heart . . ." (Matt. 22:37). If the greatest commandment is to love God with all of my heart, then the greatest sin must be to love God with any less than all of my heart!

Jesus commended the Ephesian church for their diligent activity, their sound doctrine, their separated lifestyle, and their endurance. But He grieved that they had left their "first love" (Rev. 2:4). He warned that if they did not remember, repent, and restore their devotion to Him, He would render them useless by causing their light to no longer shine.

Revival brings a new hatred for sin.

In the manifest presence of a holy God, we come to see ourselves as we really are and to detest every deviation from His righteous character in our lives. Over and over again in God's Word, we read of men who were deemed spiritual by others, but who came to see the deceitfulness and wickedness of their own flesh when they came face to face with God.

Isaiah was a man chosen of God to communicate His truth to a godless generation. Early in his ministry, Isaiah was given a vision of the exalted, reigning, thrice-holy Lord of Hosts. By contrast, Isaiah saw himself to be utterly defiled, unworthy, and in desperate need of cleansing at the altar.

Job was a righteous man who honored and worshiped God. But intense suffering revealed a root of self-righteousness and pride in his view of himself. After listening silently to Job's lengthy defenses of himself and his righteousness, God told Job to stop talking and to listen as God revealed His character and His ways. From that awful, blinding encounter with God, Job emerged with a radically altered view of himself. "I have heard of Thee by the hearing of the ear: but now mine eye seeth Thee. Wherefore I abhor myself, and repent in dust and ashes" (Job 42:5,6).

The church today seems to have little fear of God. Few of us can honestly say that we "abhor that which is evil; [and] cleave to that which is good" (Rom. 12:9). In crusade after crusade, we counsel with professing believers who are indulging themselves in fleshly lifestyles, clinging tenaciously to pet sins, and ignoring clear-cut commands of God's Word. In the past several years, I have observed a growing tendency among Christians to treat known sin casually. Revival requires that we see ourselves and our sin as God does, and that we cooperate with Him in rooting out of our lives all that is unholy. A revived church is a pure church.

Revival brings a new joy in our walk with God.

The psalmist reminds us that God revives us that we may "rejoice in Thee" (Ps. 85:6). In the unrevived state of the church, we derive our joy from circumstances, programs, entertainment, and things that appeal to our flesh. However, true and lasting joy is only to be found in the presence of God and through Jesus, who sits at the right hand of the Father (Ps. 16:11). Nehemiah 8:17 points out that one of the by-products of the great revival before the water gate was "very great gladness."

Joy, laughter, and singing are signs of a revived people. No wonder the psalmist exclaimed, "When the LORD turned again the captivity of Zion, we were like them that dream. Then was our mouth filled with laughter, and our tongue with singing . . ." (Ps. 126:1,2).

Generally, in the first week or so of our crusades, people are reluctant to really sing out—which isn't very surprising, considering how empty and unhappy the average Christian seems to be. But as people begin to be emptied of sin and filled with the Spirit, the new inner fulness begins to express itself in their singing. You no longer have to depend on a soloist or a team of singers. People can't help but make their own music to the Lord. Nothing can quench the overflowing joy that results when people's hearts are purified, their consciences are cleared, and their innermost beings are filled with the Holy Spirit.

Revival brings a new love for others.

Those who have been forgiven much, love much (Luke 7:47). Believers who have come face to face with their own sinfulness and have been forgiven by the grace of God no longer find it difficult to love others. Love for God's people is the natural overflow of love for God. In a revived church, bitterness, grudges, critical spirits, anger, and conflict are replaced by genuine love, forgiveness, humility, and oneness.

Nowhere is this product of revival seen more clearly than in our homes. Malachi prophesied that in preparation for the coming of Jesus, the hearts of the fathers would be turned to their children and the hearts of the children would be turned to their fathers (Mal. 4:6). Revival, like the filling of the Spirit, is evidenced in submissive wives, loving husbands, and obedient children.

Revival brings a new freedom.

The Old Testament repeatedly describes revival as the turning back of captivity (Pss. 85:1; 126:1; Isa. 61:1-3).

The account of the raising of Lazarus from the dead in John 11 illustrates the freedom that comes with genuine revival. Lazarus went through three distinct stages. First, when Jesus arrived in Bethany, Lazarus was dead, a picture of the non-Christian. Then Jesus commanded, "Lazarus, come forth!" Lazarus did so, but the Scripture tells us that he was still bound by the yards of grave clothes and layers of sticky spices that had been wrapped around him for burial. He was alive, but he was bound. What a picture of the average Christian—alive, but bound! For all practical purposes, there is very little difference between this unrevived believer, and the unbeliever. But Jesus did not leave Lazarus in that condition. He spoke the word, "Loose him and let him go!" And that is exactly what God does for us in times of revival. He sets us free!

Early one morning during a crusade, I heard a knock on my trailer door. When I opened the door, the man who stood outside burst into tears and said, "I'm free! I'm free!" So often these are among the first words to come out of the mouths of those who have been revived. What do they mean? They mean that in their unrevived state they were prisoners. They were in bondage to sin, guilt, bitterness, moral impurity, or habits they could not break. But Jesus came to set prisoners free and to loose the bonds of sin.

Through Jesus' death and resurrection and the power of His indwelling life, the prison doors have been thrown open, the key has been thrown away, and we are eternally free! Words cannot describe the sense of release that comes when believers discover and appropriate the truth that sets them free.

Revival brings a new power.

The unrevived church is a powerless church. All the results it produces can be explained in terms of natural ability, effort, and energy. The late Dr. J. Edwin Orr, a historian of revival, pointed out, "In the unrevived state of the church, saints go racing to find sinners. But in the revived state of the church, sinners will come racing to find the Savior!"

A lost world cannot help but feel the impact of genuine revival in the church. In fact, virtually every social reform movement, every evangelistic thrust, and every missionary movement in history has been born out of revival.

In the wake of real revival, timid, self-conscious believers who never before dared to speak of their faith to the lost, will discover anointing and power for witness. Over and over again, I have watched God loose the tongues of young people, housewives, businessmen, and—yes—even preachers, to witness with freedom and boldness.

The revived church is a church endued with supernatural power from on high. That is why the oft-heard cry of the Welsh Revival was, "Bend the church to save the world."

The early church was known for the signs and wonders of God at work in their midst. Empowered and energized by the Holy Spirit against incredible opposition and odds, they soon reached the whole known world with the gospel of Jesus. The revived church is a church where God is releasing His supernatural power.

A MODERN MIRACLE

I will always remember February 1985 as the month God chose to visit a little Midwestern town with one of the most remarkable manifestations of His power that I had seen in many years.

When my family and I pulled into town that blustery Saturday afternoon, we could not have begun to imagine all that God had in store for us.

The crusade was scheduled for two weeks. However, God had different plans! After four weeks in that church, during which God moved in an extraordinary way, several churches in a nearby town across the state line spontaneously asked if we would bring the crusade to their area. On three days' notice, they decided to cancel everything on their calendars, and the crusade continued for another three weeks.

Some time later, the pastor of one of those churches summarized the impact of the crusade on his life, family, ministry, and community. The following is an excerpt from his report:

Revival Fires in the Midwest

God visited our church in a way that was totally unexpected and unplanned by us. The staff and I had known for some time that our church and community needed a visitation from God. We prayed for revival, but none of us really knew what we were asking God to do. We received more than we expected—we got what we needed!

Cottage prayer meetings were established prior to the crusade, and a handful began to earnestly seek God for revival. In the services prior to the crusade, we witnessed some initial stirrings of the Spirit, but nothing like what we were to experience in the next several weeks.

The team rolled into town on a cold Indiana day, February 2, 1985. February is not the normal time to schedule a revival, but this proves that God was the One making the schedule—not us. As the team began to unload their equipment, I remember wondering what God had in store for us. Little did we realize that the team would be with us for five Sundays and that the crusade would continue in our area for seven weeks.

During the first two weeks of the crusade, the Holy Spirit stuck the plow of conviction deeper and deeper into our hearts. Although it was painful at first, it was a vital part of the process of true revival. If there is not first a breaking of hard hearts, then planting seeds of truth will result in no real harvest.

Prayer

If there was one thing that marked a major difference between this crusade and other meetings we have had, it was the priority placed on prayer.

From the opening service of the crusade, Del emphasized that the team did not bring revival with them, that no amount of preaching and singing could make revival happen, and that we must fervently cry out to God in prayer.

Challenged by a vision of what God could do if we sought Him with all of our hearts, our church was transformed into a "house of prayer."

In almost every crusade service, we took time out as a congregation to go to our knees. We joined our hearts together in one accord to worship and praise the Lord and to intercede on behalf of our homes, our church, and our community.

Conviction

One of the marked characteristics of this revival was the intense conviction of God's Spirit in individual hearts and lives. God was intent on purifying and purging His people. And so, like a great prairie fire, the presence and holiness of God consumed everything in its way. As God began to turn on the heat of His conviction, sin that had been hidden or tolerated for years began to be exposed. God made people miserable over their sinful condition and brought many to the place that they would rather die than to go on in their sin.

One after another, hearts that had long been stubborn, rebellious, and proud were melted and conquered in His presence. Many nights the prayer room and even the main service were filled with people earnestly confessing and weeping over their sin. After one service, a pastor shared that God had so gripped him with conviction that he could hardly breathe or stand to his feet.

Those who thought they could escape from the hand of God by staying away from the crusade services found that God's conviction over unconfessed sin, unbroken wills, and unsurrendered lives pursued them to their schools, places of business, and homes. Over and over again, we heard testimonies of people who wrestled with God through sleepless nights, until they finally could resist no longer and waved the "white flag of surrender."

The conviction that moved like a tidal wave through our town and then into nearby communities was obviously not the result of man-made manipulation or emotional preaching. Rather, the Word of God and the presence of the Spirit of God reached into the hearts of men and caused them to be overwhelmed with their need to get right with God and with others. What we saw was a powerful confirmation of the truth. "Is not My Word like as a fire? saith the LORD; and like a hammer that breaketh the rock in pieces?" (Jer. 23:29).

Reconciliation

As God worked to convict and cleanse hearts, people began to realize that it was impossible to be right with God and not be right with one another. The emphasis of the first week of the crusade was on having a pure heart before God. Much of the second week focused on having a clear conscience before men.

God's people committed themselves to make right the offenses of the past, in their homes, in the body of Christ, and in the community. Many were set free from years of unresolved conflict and bitterness as they humbled themselves, confessed their wrong, and sought forgiveness.

We saw people whose sin had affected the whole church take responsibility for their sin, stand before the church, confess their sin, and seek forgiveness from the church. Some of the sweetest outpourings of love took place as the church eagerly forgave them and rushed in to restore them.

One of the greatest public demonstrations of this revival took place on the night that thirty to forty people in our church drove across town to another church that had split off ten years earlier to ask forgiveness for their bitterness, wrong responses, and pride in the midst of that conflict.

The man who was the chairman of our deacon board at the time of the split stood before that congregation and quietly, humbly, brokenly sought forgiveness, on his own behalf and on behalf of our entire church. He told how he had lived a lie for all of these years, going through all the motions of Christianity, but inwardly filled with pride, anger, and resentment. He said, "In the midst of all that turmoil, I never once suggested that we pray together and seek God for healing, wisdom, and grace."

That night grown men who had avoided each other for years ended up in each others' arms, weeping and expressing love and forgiveness. The impact of this incident on the community and on the families involved is still being felt. Tears of grief, brokenness, and repentance were replaced with tears of overflowing joy and love, as barriers of guilt, selfishness, and pride were torn down between God's people.

Restoration

The most needed and thrilling restoration of broken relationships during the crusade was between husbands and wives. Satan had established a stronghold of broken marriages in our church and community. It seemed that every time we turned around, there was another marriage falling apart. It became obvious that God could not trust His glory to our church until we agreed with Him about the seriousness of what was taking place in our homes and took steps to restore His standard of the permanence of marriage.

At the beginning of the crusade, the Life Action team and our church staff targeted about five marriages that were broken apart by divorce or were clearly headed in that direction. As the crusade progressed, several other couples were added to that list. In response to fervent prayer, God began to move in each of these marriages.

We found ourselves on the front lines of a fierce war with the forces of hell, as we attempted to help these mates take personal responsibility for years of selfishness, bitterness, moral impurity, and temporal values. In one case after another, as the Holy Spirit performed "heart surgery," we watched blame, anger, resentment, and rebellion turn to forgiveness, humility, love, and restored oneness. These marriages are now becoming display cases for God's glory in our church.

Salvation

As believers got honest about their true spiritual condition, confessed their sin, and were cleansed, set free, and filled with the Spirit, lost people came under conviction of their need for a Savior.

As people got right with God and with one another, they had a new boldness to share Christ with others. One attorney was impressed of God to begin each day in his law office with a brief devotional message from God's Word for his staff.

A visiting pastor's wife sat in the services for two-and-one-half weeks, miserable, under conviction, and refusing to yield some areas of her life to God. Finally, God broke her and she went to the prayer room to obey God. God restored to her the joy of His salvation, and the next morning she led a lady to the Lord over the phone.

Many lost people in our town have heard a lot about Jesus. Now they are beginning to see the reality of Jesus in the lives of revived believers, and they are thirsty for what they are seeing.

We soon discovered that it was impossible to contain the reviving power of God within the four walls of one local church. Word of what God was doing quickly spread through our town and then into nearby communities. Transformed lives were the vehicle most used by God to reach others. What took place in the actual crusade services was just the tip of the iceberg of all that God was doing in our area.

The intense fire of God's presence moved supernaturally to impact our entire community. As the revival spread, churches of other denominations were affected and Christians in nearby communities were brought under conviction. Classes were suspended in Christian schools as God took over the student body. Only eternity will reveal all the lives that were affected by this revival.

During the last week of the crusade, one of the Life Action staff members related the following thoughts:

"A few moments ago, I drove across the bridge into town. As I came to the stop sign at the edge of town, I was overwhelmed with a sense of the presence of God. I began to weep as I realized that Jesus had visited this town with His glory. For fifteen years, I have prayed and sought God for this kind of gracious visitation. I am humbled and deeply grateful that God has allowed me to see this manifestation of His glory."

Chapter 9

There Is Always a Price Tag

Revival does not come easily. There is always a price to pay. Rick Lawson was an engineering supervisor with top-level security clearance on his job when our crusade began in Fort Worth, Texas. During the crusade Rick was saved and became concerned about his need to clear his conscience over the fact that he had lied when he filled out his security clearance forms.

"I remember lying awake at night," Rick said. "I couldn't get the whole thing out of my mind. At first, I tried to appease God by taking care of some smaller things in my life, but even after I got those right, I still couldn't live with myself."

Finally, Rick told his wife that if he was going to be right with God, he would have to resubmit his paperwork, that it could lead to a full FBI investigation, and that he might lose his job over it. (The company for which Rick worked is one of the largest defense contractors for the U. S. Government.) When he applied for the job, he had lied about his use of drugs while he was a student and the form made it clear that any willful false statement could result in "imprisonment of up to ten years and a fine of up to $10,000."

"I had used drugs repeatedly while I was in college and on a few isolated occasions after that," Rick admitted. "But I knew that if I told the truth on the application, I probably wouldn't get the job."

After a few more days of struggle, Rick finally decided to resubmit the paperwork. "I attached a note explaining that I had given my life to Jesus Christ and felt I needed to confess to them that I had lied when I originally filled out my security forms," Rick explained. "I asked them to forgive me and told them how sorry I was that I had lied. I can still remember walking down the hall with that envelope in my hand. Satan kept harassing me with the thought that if there is no God, you have blown your job and your life for nothing.

"It was almost a week before I heard anything. Finally, my boss called me into his office. The Director of Security was there.

"'The Navy has asked that you be suspended pending an investigation,' he said. 'I will need to take your security badge.'"

Rick was allowed to continue working and even supervising his crew, but he no longer had security clearance into the building. He was given a desk in the hallway and found himself faced with constant opportunities to explain what God had done in his life!

"People told me I was crazy trusting the Security Department to handle my case," Rick explained. "But I told them that they were not the one I was trusting—I was trusting God."

Rick continued as the supervisor on the project for the next several months despite the limitations placed upon him. Hundreds of people became aware of his testimony and were moved by it. In the fall, there was a full Defense Department investigation and the interviewer turned out to be a fellow believer. "More time passed and my boss became fearful that the investigation might drag on indefinitely," Rick said. "I felt torn between Christ and the world. How could I have expected them to understand? Then my boss called me back to tell me the FBI had cleared me and that I could complete the project."

Rick finished his assignment and has now been reassigned to another area with an even better situation for him and his family. "I have never regretted what I did," Rick says today. "The utter helplessness of being dependent on God alone was exactly what I needed."

But God wasn't through dealing with Rick Lawson. A second step of obedience involved clearing his conscience with Oklahoma State University, where he had attended college. He had stolen some books and a calculator worth about $250. He sent a check back to the school along with a note similar to the one he had submitted to Security.

"About a week later," Rick said, "a writer from the *Okla-legion*, the school paper at OSU, called our house and asked permission to print my story, because it was so rare for somebody to do what I had done. When the story came out in the school paper, they even printed the note that I had written."

The story was later reprinted in the local newspaper and in the *Daily Oklahoman*, a statewide paper. Rick met with his pastor before leaving on a business trip, and they prayed that God would use all of this to His glory.

"Then I left on the trip," Rick said, "and I bought a *USA Today* newspaper in the Philadelphia airport, only to find that my story had been picked up by the wire service, and had been re-printed on page two! It was really a humbling experience to realize you had just confessed to the whole country."

Decisions like these became the turning point in Rick Lawson's life. "When I started being obedient to God," Rick explained, "the Lord began teaching me more and more. My wife became secure in our relationship because I was taking the lead spiritually. We began to love each other more deeply, and our relationship grew even stronger."

SPIRITUAL SURGERY

Who of us can look at the products of revival and not desire that they might be true of us? Yet anything of value costs, and the greater the value, the greater the price. In our instant generation, we want gain without pain. This simply is not possible in spiritual matters. The thought of surgery is not pleasant. None of us would schedule it unnecessarily, but if we know surgery is the only way to restore health, then we are willing to endure the pain. No woman looks forward to the labor pains of childbirth, but she is willing to go through the suffering, in anticipation of the joy of a new life.

In the spiritual realm, there can be no life without death; there can be no resurrection without a cross; there can be no honor without humility; there can be no healing without hurt.

Revival is not cheap. It will not be experienced by those who merely read about it and wish for it. The rich fruits of revival will come to those who are willing to pay the price.

Thirst

God's Word promises, "I will pour water upon him that is thirsty, and floods upon the dry ground" (Isa. 44:3). Only those who are willing to acknowledge the parched condition of their lives and who recognize their desperate need for God qualify to receive the refreshing of His Spirit. Not until I am so thirsty that I simply cannot go on as I am, will I draw upon the riches of His grace to meet that need.

Several chapters later Isaiah issues an invitation to those who are thirsty: "Ho, every one that thirsteth, come ye to the waters, and he that hath no money; come ye, buy, and eat" (Isa. 55:1). Have you ever wondered how those who have no money can buy provisions to meet their need? The prophet simply illustrated the reality that provisions to meet my spirit's needs cannot be purchased with money. Rather, I must come to God and offer Him all that I have—my poverty, my emptiness, and my need. In exchange, He gives to me His wealth, His fulness, His abundance.

At a dramatic point in His earthly ministry, the Lord Jesus stood and cried out, "If any man thirst, let him come unto Me, and drink. He that believeth on Me, as the scripture hath said, out of his belly shall flow rivers of living water" (John 7:37,38).

I remember the chancellor of a Christian university who so desperately wanted to see revival sweep his campus that he prayed in his car all night at the entrance gate to the campus. No wonder nearly three hundred students came to Christ in that crusade.

Patience

Judging by most of our church calendars, we want revival, but we want it on our schedule and we want it fast! The days of revival meetings scheduled for six weeks or more are long past. This is the era of four-day revival crusades, of mini-revivals. We think we're making the ultimate sacrifice if we schedule a crusade for a whole week, much less two or three weeks. Our programs must go on. People are busy. We just don't have time.

Over and over again, God's Word reveals that God is found by those who are willing to wait for Him. "I will hear what God the LORD will speak" (Ps. 85:8). "Ye shall seek Me, and find Me, when ye shall search for Me with all your heart" (Jer. 29:13). The sad fact is that most of us are simply too busy to stop, to be quiet, to listen to God, to give Him our undivided attention, and to seek for Him with all our hearts. The Bible reminds us that we cannot imagine what is in store for us if we wait upon God (see Isa. 64:4).

Obedience

We cannot expect God to bless us and fill us if we are not willing to bow before Him as Lord in every area of our lives. Partial obedience, delayed obedience, and surface obedience to impress others are not acceptable to God. He is looking for men and women who will respond with instant, complete, wholehearted, and joyous obedience each time He speaks. In order to experience revival, most of us do not need to hear more truths, we simply need to obey that which we already know.

There was an ancient oriental custom in which a monarch would send his messenger ahead to announce the coming of the king. In preparation for his arrival, the king's subjects would build a highway. The valleys had to be filled in, and the high places had to be brought down. The crooked places were straightened, and the stones and roots removed from the rough places. When the highway had been prepared, the king would come.

My friend, King Jesus wants to come visit His people! He wants to fill our lives and our churches with His glorious presence. But we must prepare the way. In the closing verse of Psalm 85, we read, "Righteousness shall go before Him; and shall set us in the way of His steps." The prophet Isaiah cried, "Prepare ye the way of the LORD, make straight in the desert a highway for our God, And the glory of the LORD shall be revealed" (Isa. 40:3,5).

Obedience is not always easy; in fact, it is often costly. Richard Magnussen, a Canadian furniture manufacturer, paid thousands of dollars as restitution for stealing designs from other manufacturers, even though the practice is common in his industry. Then God dealt with him about the fact that four times a year, at furniture shows, he was open on Sundays. Those four Sundays normally accounted for some 60 percent of his business, so when he made the decision not to open his display on the Lord's Day, he knew it might cost him his business. In this case, God honored Richard's decision in a tangible way. Instead of costing him sales, buyers have been impressed by his stand and his business has been growing rapidly in a soft market.

When I think of the cost of obedience, I am reminded of the young man in Oklahoma who wrecked his truck to collect $7,000 in insurance and was convicted that he needed to make restitution. "That's a lot of money," a friend suggested.

"No amount of money is too much to get right with God," he replied.

I remember another man in Houston, Texas, who admitted, "I've been more faithful in paying my taxes than my tithe. I've honored Caesar, but not God." He later paid $22,000 in back tithes to the Lord. I also remember the dentist in Oklahoma City who paid $26,000 in back taxes after he was convicted that he had never reported his cash income.

Obedience was costly for the cat burglar in Des Moines, Iowa, who had broken into over one hundred homes, stealing thousands of dollars worth of goods. He had since been saved, but had never gone back to make restitution. When God moved in his heart, he went back house by house, asking forgiveness and working out a repayment schedule. "It became a perpetual opportunity for grace and humility in my life," he acknowledged.

I remember the young divorced mother in Lincoln, Nebraska, who had burned her trailer to collect the insurance money. When God convicted her, she told herself, "I'll go to jail if I confess this." But her conscience responded, "You're already in jail!" She did what was right, and the insurance company allowed her to work out a long-term repayment plan and did not file any charges against her. A year later, she wrote and said her estranged husband, moved by what she had done, had come home, sought reconciliation, and remarried her.

In another instance, one man actually did go to prison as a result of clearing his conscience with Canadian authorities. For years he had lived in the United States as a fugitive from the law. Finally, under deep conviction, he turned himself in and was sent to prison for many months. But as we later talked with his wife, she expressed the enormous joy she felt because at long last her husband, though physically incarcerated, was truly free.

Another believer, whose husband was killed several years ago in the Iraqi bombing of the *U.S.S. Stark* in the Persian Gulf, knows that obedience is not always easy. In the midst of revival, this widow was challenged to make her greatest investment in the area where she had the greatest potential for bitterness. Therefore, she sold her home, moved to Iraq, and ministered to people in the very town from which the planes that killed her husband had been launched. Today she is back in the United States ministering to Iraqi students.

Whenever God sends revival, it is because His people are willing to pay whatever price is necessary to be a holy bride.

NEED FOR HOLINESS

Holiness is the one quality which marks people of God as different from the world. It is also the one essential for power in the church.

Today's church is not powerful because it is not holy. We must be holy because we are the dwelling place of a holy God. An unholy temple is not a fit place for our God.

We must be holy because we have been purchased and washed by a holy Savior. We are not our own. We have been bought with the infinite price of His life-blood.

We must be holy because we have been justified for the purpose of being sanctified. Christ "loved the church, and gave Himself for it; That He might sanctify and cleanse it with the washing of water by the word . . ." (Eph. 5:25,26). To be holy is our calling. God's purpose for the church is not necessarily to make us happy, but to make us holy.

We must be holy because we are the bride of Christ. Paul wrote to the carnal Corinthian church, "I am jealous over you with godly jealousy: for I have espoused you to one husband, that I may present you as a chaste virgin to Christ" (2 Cor. 11:2). We have been engaged to a holy Christ. As a bride adorned in white speaks of a woman who kept herself chaste and pure for her husband, so as the bride of Christ, we long to stand before Him one day at the marriage of the Lamb, "arrayed in fine linen, clean and white . . . [which] is the righteousness of saints" (Rev. 19:8).

What does it mean to be holy?

To be a holy bride is to be clean through and through. It surely includes being blameless in every matter that is visible to others—in conduct, speech, dress, and in habits and lifestyle. But holiness runs far deeper than that which can be evaluated by men. True holiness is produced in the heart of the believer by the indwelling Holy Spirit. It means being clean inside, where only God sees. It means to have only holy attitudes, values, thoughts, and motives. To be holy is to be like Jesus—"holy, harmless, undefiled, separate from sinners" (Heb. 7:26). It is to be without spot, pretense, or guile.

Unfortunately, all too often the church in the twentieth century has measured herself by the world's standards and has been satisfied with being relatively holy. That is to say, by comparison to the world, we think ourselves to be in pretty good shape. But there is no such thing as relative holiness. Holiness is not a matter of degrees. The church is either holy or it is unholy.

What things defile the temple of God?

We might rightly say that any deviation from God's holy character and any violation of His holy Word defiles the body of Christ. But the Scripture highlights a number of specific sins in the body that particularly grieve the Spirit of God.

In the Old Testament, there are numerous specific instances where God judged His people for the sins of idolatry, murmuring, discontentment, covetousness, unbelief, and rebellion against God-ordained authority. Whether the sin was committed by a leader, a single individual, or the entire congregation, a high toll was always exacted for defiling the nation to which God had entrusted His glory.

The apostle Paul frequently wrote to the New Testament churches about sins that contaminated the body. He warned them to put away anything that could possibly offend a holy God and grieve His Holy Spirit.

For example, doctrinal impurity of every type was dangerous and not to be tolerated. Paul knew that ultimately doctrine determines practice; false doctrine inevitably results in wrong living (see 1 Cor. 15:33; Gal. 5:8,9). He taught that those entrusted with the spiritual leadership in the church have a responsibility to safeguard the church from teachings or philosophies that are unscriptural.

Paul also cautioned against disorderly conduct in the church, giving specific instructions about personal behavior, the use of spiritual gifts, the roles of men and women in public services, and the importance of holy living.

Then Paul expressed grave concern over contentious members of the church who were guilty of creating divisions in the body. These schisms were invariably rooted in pride. He chastised those who made absolutes out of personal preferences, as well as those who exalted mere men over Christ, the Head of the church.

Paul was especially severe in his warnings against tolerating any type of moral impurity in the church. He wrote, "But fornication, and all uncleanness, or covetousness, let it not be once named among you, as becometh saints" (Eph. 5:3). In other words, since you are saints, live like saints!

What are the consequences of unholiness in the church?

An unholy church will lose its sense of God's presence and destroy its ability to fellowship with Him. "Blessed are the pure in heart: for they shall see God" (Matt. 5:8). "Follow . . . holiness, without which no man shall see the Lord" (Heb. 12:14). A holy preacher of a past generation reminded his hearers that "the fellowship of heaven is not enjoyed where the leaven of hell is endured."

An unholy church is an impotent church. Sin that is not dealt with in God's way robs the church of the supernatural power of God. On the eve of their passage over Jordan into the Promised Land, Joshua did not call a committee meeting to determine the best strategy for reaching the other side. He did not schedule a rally with a popular vocal artist to get the people psyched up for the trek. He did not even call a prayer meeting. Rather, he exhorted the people to: "Sanctify yourselves: for tomorrow the LORD will do wonders among you" (Josh. 3:5). Only unwillingness to part with known sin could limit the mighty hand of God. Just a few days later, in the battle of Ai, the Israelites learned this truth at the cost of thirty-six lives.

An unholy church forfeits its distinctive testimony and witness in the world. When God told Moses that the rebellious nation would have to go into the Promised Land without His presence, Moses protested: "For wherein shall it be known here that I and Thy people have found grace in Thy sight? is it not in that Thou goest with us? so shall we be separated, I and Thy people, from all the people that are upon the face of the earth" (Ex. 33:16). Apart from practical, genuine holiness, we cannot enjoy the manifest presence and glory of God in our midst. And apart from His presence, we are really no different than any other social club or religious institution.

How can purity be maintained in the body of Christ?

There is both a personal and a corporate responsibility for preserving the purity of the church.

In 1 Corinthians 11, Paul deals with the need for each individual believer to be cleansed from all known sin. First, he says, "Examine [yourself]" (v. 28). Honestly and humbly compare your life to the unchanging, absolute standard of Scripture and to the heart and life of Jesus. Be thorough. Do not allow even one little sin to escape the scrutiny of His holiness and the searchlight of His Spirit. Then "Judge [yourself]" (v. 31). Agree with God that every sin is an act of cosmic rebellion against the Lord of the universe. Acknowledge the seriousness of every unholy thought, word, or action. Be quick to repent of the sin, to place it under the blood of Christ, and to utterly forsake and renounce it.

However, it is not sufficient that we should deal merely with our personal sins. We also shoulder an awesome responsibility to preserve holiness in the church. We are all members of one body. When one member sins, we all bear the burden and reproach of his failure. That is why we must understand and be committed to the scriptural process of restorative discipline toward sinning brothers.

By and large, the church in recent generations has been unwilling to take responsibility for dealing with sin in its midst. The path of least resistance is to let these things go. To become involved in the process of discipline and restoration requires considerable time and effort, as well as willingness to lay our own reputation on the altar. It requires that we be willing to forsake all known sin in our own lives. It may not be the easiest path or the most convenient, but it is God's way of holiness. C. H. Spurgeon, the great nineteenth-century English preacher, said:

> The toleration of sin in the church soon leads to the excusing of it, and then to the free indulgence of it, and to the bringing in of other sins yet more foul. Sin is like the bale of goods which came

from the east to this city in the olden time, which brought the pest in it. Probably it was but a small bale, but yet it contained in it the deaths of hundreds of the inhabitants of London. In those days one piece of rag carried the infection into a whole town. So, if you knowingly permit one sin in a church, none can tell the extent to which that evil may ultimately go. The church, therefore, is to be purged of evil as diligently as possible.

The price of revival is repentance and obedience. The condition that results is holiness, and the effect it produces is spiritual power and conviction. Nothing less is worthy of our Holy Father, whose glory fills heaven and earth. Nothing less is worthy of our Holy Savior, who shed His blood to redeem us from sin. Nothing less is worthy of His Holy Spirit, whose temple we are.

Chapter 10

When the Glory Returns

It had been an exhausting day. The hot sun beat down on the parched earth. The crowd sat under the cloudless sky for what seemed like an eternity—silent spectators in this playoff between Baal and Jehovah. Jehovah's side was hopelessly outnumbered—the odds, 850 to 1 in favor of Baal.

Silently, they watched and waited and wondered as the prophets of Baal tried first one tactic and then another to persuade the god of lightning and fire to prove himself and send fire from heaven. They pled; they appealed. Unsuccessful, they began to cry out more earnestly, to cajole, to demand that Baal heed them and send fire. Still no answer. Still no fire.

Undaunted, they persisted in leaping upon the altar and cutting themselves until the blood flowed—desperate, vain attempts to prove their sincerity to Baal and to see some evidence—any evidence—of spiritual reality. But there was no sign of fire from heaven—not even a spark. In fact, there had been no movement of any kind in the heavens for more than three years—no fire, no rain, no voice, no reality. Weary with the exercise in futility, desire turned to disappointment and finally defeat.

At this point in 1 Kings 18, we cannot help noticing some striking similarities to the church in our day. The great problem in the contemporary church is that despite its size and activity, there is no real expression of the glory of God's presence.

By and large, we are not lacking activity, fervor, or attempts to obtain spiritual power. To the contrary, our church calendars are bulging with services, retreats, conferences, and programs. We are making lots of noise. We are busy, earnest, and perhaps sincere, but still there is deafening silence in the heavens. *There is no fire.* It's not that we are not trying. We are. But apparently, all of our programs, promotions, meetings, buses, budgets, baptisms, committees, and conventions have failed to produce the one thing we need most desperately—fire from heaven.

While the spiritual leaders and activists are busily trying to produce sparks, the average church member sits back with the rest of the world—waiting, watching, and wondering where the fire is.

CALLING DOWN THE FIRE

Into the arena steps a solitary figure. He has been a fugitive from the king whose wrath he incurred three years earlier. One would expect him to cower in the presence of the offended monarch. After all, he stands to lose his life. But no, he is secure, assured, and bold.

Now he is calling to the people to listen. They gather around him skeptically. This man has always been something of an oddity—a real contrast to other religious leaders of his day. His has always been a minority voice. His message cuts across the grain of what is traditional and palatable. His challenge to get off the fence and take a public stand for Baal or Jehovah makes the average person uncomfortable. He would rather not commit himself.

Now he directs their attention to the altar of Jehovah. Unused for many years, it is in a state of disrepair. One by one, he selects twelve large stones and constructs an altar. He prepares the sacrifice and places it on the altar.

Then he catches them off guard. Turning to the crowd, he directs them to fill four barrels with water and pour it on the sacrifice.

What? Has he lost his mind? Anyone knows wet wood will not burn! Even more importantly, doesn't this strange man know that it hasn't rained for over three years? Nevertheless, they follow his orders.

Then a short, simple prayer, and . . . *fire!* No matches. No kerosene. No magic tricks. No gyrations. No pretending. Just fire. Real fire. Fire that licks up the water and utterly consumes the sacrifice, the wood, the stones—even the dust on the ground. Fire from heaven. The fire of God.

What is the fire of God?

I do not know of any greater need in the church today than for the fire of God to fall. When we refer to the fire of God, we are talking about the manifest presence and glory of God. We are talking about the supernatural power of God. We are talking about services that are more than just nice meetings with nice music and nice preaching. We are talking about results that cannot be explained in terms of human effort. We are talking about that which man cannot program, manipulate, plan, or make happen. We are talking about something more than the ordinary operation of the Holy Spirit in the lives of His people. We are talking about the extraordinary outpouring of His Spirit that reveals His glory in our lives and in His church.

What does the fire do?

When the fire falls, we see God for who He really is. Both the Old and New Testaments reveal God to be a God of fire. At Mount Sinai, where the law was given, God revealed Himself with lightnings and thunderings and voices. Then, in the last book of the Bible, the apostle John was given a glimpse into the throne room of heaven. Out of that throne "proceeded lightnings and thunderings and voices" (Rev. 4:5).

When the fire falls, God takes over His church. When God shows up, people are more comfortable on their faces than in their pews. When the fire falls, it consumes everything that is unholy, earthly, and temporal.

The fire of God purifies, purges, melts, and devours, "For our God is a consuming fire" (Heb. 12:29). God is like a refiner's fire (Mal. 3:2) that brings impurities to the surface and exposes and consumes them.

When the fire falls, sin is judged and dealt with thoroughly and uncompromisingly—not just the obvious sins of the flesh, but subtle, secret sins of the spirit as well. Masks of respectability are pulled off, pretenses stripped away, and the souls of men laid bare before the gaze of an all-seeing, all-knowing God.

When the fire comes, there is deep, heart conviction and grief over sin. The intense searchlight of God's holiness makes things once thought acceptable, to suddenly become abhorrent. Indifference is turned to mourning. A casual attitude toward sin is replaced by brokenness and genuine repentance.

When the fire falls, the efforts and works of believers are tested. Much of what appeared to be spiritual activity is exposed to be nothing more than fleshly effort that is consumed as wood, hay, and stubble.

When the fire falls, our traditional methods and programs are all yielded to His Lordship and the Holy Spirit begins to preside in reality over the workings and operation of His church.

When the fire falls, there is power, there is life, there is purity, there is spontaneity, there is reality.

Where is the fire of God today? Where is the evidence of His presence and power? Where is the sense of awe, of wonder, of fear in His presence? Where are the tears of brokenness and contrition? Where are lost people falling on their faces, overcome by the reality of God's presence in the midst of His people? What church in your community is known to have the fire of God? In what Sunday School class, home, mom, dad, or teenager is the fire present?

Why don't we have the fire?

In many cases, we do not have the fire of God because we don't think we need it. We are content to live without His glory. For the most part, our nation, churches, homes, and lives are devoid of the glory and power of God. When asked to state our needs, we speak of needing bigger buildings, more money, more volunteers, better staff, or more equipment. Why can't we see that our real need is for God Himself?

We sinned against God, and He withdrew His manifest presence from us, but our eyes have grown accustomed to the darkness. We are used to functioning in our own effort. Hardly anyone questions the authenticity of the results. Someone has said that if the Holy Spirit were taken out of the average church, 95 percent of the program would keep right on going.

We have become blind to our true spiritual condition and need. Like the Laodicean church, we think we are "rich, and increased with goods, and have need of nothing" (Rev. 3:17).

I hear Christian leaders today speak of how Christianity is flourishing. Others insist we are in the throes of revival. If that is the case, then why is every form of moral impurity rampant in our evangelical, Bible-preaching churches? Why is the divorce rate as high in the church as it is in the world? Why do the vast majority of Christians never introduce anyone to Christ? Why do people want a part-time, convenient, weekend Christian experience that costs them nothing? Why do pastors have to twist people's arms to get them to serve the Lord?

Why are church splits so common? Why are so many professing Christians barren, empty, hurting, and in spiritual bondage? Why is the world so utterly disinterested in what we have to offer? As long as we think we are doing all right, we will never cry out to God to send fire from heaven.

I believe another reason we do not have the fire is that we really don't want it. Oh, we say we do, but what too many of us really want is the kind of fire that draws attention to our church, packs our auditorium, increases our offerings, and solves all our problems. We don't want the fire that consumes, destroys, exposes, roots up, burns, and hurts. We are afraid of what might happen if God appeared on the scene. We want a tidy religious experience that we can control.

Furthermore, we don't want the kind of preaching that precedes revival. I have found that many people want nothing but encouragement and love from the pulpit. They don't want the truth! Preaching on sin, repentance, holiness, brokenness, or confession is considered negative. "You're putting people on a guilt trip. You'll damage their self-esteem." I wish we were half as concerned about people having a proper view of God as we are about people having a proper view of themselves! Deceived by the world, our egocentric theology has become more concerned about self-image than about God's image.

We don't have the fire of God because we don't believe it can happen today. In order to justify our impotence, we have dispensationalized away most of God's Word. "That's Old Testament!" "God doesn't work that way today." A serious study of the history of revival reveals that every revival is, in a sense, a repetition of what took place on the Day of Pentecost. The Spirit is poured out upon His people in an extraordinary way, and the manifest presence and power of God are released.

But in our concern to avoid the excesses and abuses of certain movements, we have altogether denied the possibility of a supernatural outpouring of the Holy Spirit. We don't pray for miracles because we don't really believe that God does miracles in the twentieth century!

Finally, we don't have the fire of God because we aren't willing to pay the price to get it. We want an instantaneous, costless, painless revival. We want all the positive results and benefits of revival—at little or no cost. We want gain without pain. We want the joy of new life without going through the travail of labor pains. We want healing without surgery. We want joy without mourning. We want to enter into the power of the resurrection without first suffering the agony of the cross. We want our schedules and programs and institutions to stay intact. We want minimum disruption of our plans or interference with our traditions.

Revival involves a process—a process of plowing up the hardened, uncultivated ground of our hearts, then planting the seed, and ultimately, reaping a harvest. The plowing is painful, but it cannot be circumvented, and it takes *time*. Yes, time is an unavoidable part of the price. Weekend mini-revivals may be easier to fit into our schedules, but they are unlikely to result in genuine revival.

Elijah had been in a process of preparation and purification for three and one-half years before God sent the fire. And the people of Israel had suffered the consequences of their sin for the same period of time before they got desperate enough for God to send the fire.

We're too busy to listen to God. God meets with those who wait for Him (Isa. 64:4), but we want Him to send the fire on our timetable. And He'd better be through by noon! Dear friend, God simply will not fit into our plans, our schedules, or our timetables. He is God! And He must be given the freedom to operate as He wills, on His schedule.

If God is going to send the fire, we must be willing, if necessary, to discard our man-made traditions, methods, structures, and programs to make room for Him. It's not that those things are wrong in and of themselves, but for too many of us, they have become gods. Anything that has become more essential to us than His presence is part of the price He will require.

There certainly will be no fire until the sacrifice has been offered. For the Israelites, it meant placing their water supply on the altar. God didn't need water, but when He had their water supply, then He had them. That's what He wanted all along.

I don't know what sacrifice God may require of you or your church. He may ask you to surrender your reputation and what others think of you. He may ask you to bear criticism, misunderstanding, and rejection from those whose opinions matter most to you. He may ask you to quit your job. He may ask you to put your life savings or retirement fund on the altar. Ultimately, what God really wants is the whole of our lives. When God has us on the altar, then and only then will He send fire from heaven and reveal His power to a watching world.

WHEN REVIVAL COMES

Over the years I have met countless men and women whose lives have been transformed by the fire of God's presence. I think, for example, of the powerful work of the Spirit in the life of Wayne Stanford and his wife, Gwyn. A successful businessman and a deacon in his church, Wayne later testified that he had made a conscious effort to escape the conviction of God's Spirit regarding the true spiritual condition of his life. On the third Sunday morning of a crusade, this proud, unbroken husband could run no longer. God used the biblical account of Naaman to show him his need and bring him to brokenness and repentance. That was more than ten years ago, and to this day, Wayne can hardly talk about what God did in his life without weeping. The fire of God transformed that hard, cold heart into a tender, sensitive one. Wayne recalls, "The revival that took place in my life in May of 1982 was literally an invasion by God into the heart of one of His needy children. And," he adds, "that transforming invasion is still continuing today!"

Then, I remember being in a church where we were asked to pray for an eighteen year-old boy who was absolutely unmanageable. He had run away from home, had been sent to a reform school, had run away from there, and was living in rebellion at home. As the crusade progressed, I learned why he was so rebellious. Two years earlier, his father had become sexually involved with a teenage girl in the bus ministry and then with a lady in the church choir. As a result, the boy's mother had divorced his dad. The father had then become involved in some illegal activity and had been sent to jail.

During the first week of the crusade, the dad got out of jail. The first place he went was to the church, where we "happened" to be having services. When he walked in and sat down on the back row, the church members were noticeably shocked. That night, the man came under conviction and walked to the prayer room, where the pastor counseled with him and led him to Christ. Immediately after his conversion, he realized that he needed to make things right with his family. Initially, his wife struggled to release her bitterness, but God began to soften her heart, and by the second week, they were sitting together in the services. The dad sought forgiveness from his wounded son and set out to begin repairing the damage he had done. On the final night of that crusade, we had the privilege of watching as the pastor remarried that couple, with their eighteen-year-old son standing in as best man for his dad.

I think of the wife of a church staff member, who had battled chronic depression for years. She had become withdrawn, fearful, even suicidal because of areas of her past that she had not been willing to deal with. Even extended Christian psychiatric counseling had not been successful. However, when she obeyed God and cleared her conscience, all those symptoms disappeared.

It is easy today to hide behind all kinds of labels like "co-dependent," "dysfunctional," or "hyperactive." But true freedom comes when we admit our sin (that is confession) and when we take responsibility for it (that is repentance). When those two steps occur, God will unleash His power in our lives and in our churches.

In some instances, the fire of God falls not just on one life, but on a corporate group of believers. I will never forget the time God moved on the hearts of the pastor and people of a church in southern Texas. An ugly church split had occurred six years earlier, leaving many people hurt and embittered. The entire community was aware of the conflict and its consequences were still being felt. Even though the current pastor had come after the split, he felt the need to lead his people in confessing their wrong attitudes and actions to the other churches in the community. After much prayer, the pastor and deacons led the people in inviting the other local churches that had been affected by the split to a special reconciliation service.

The church decided to take out a full-page ad in the local newspaper. They invited all former members to attend this service and asked the city's forgiveness for gendering a spirit of gossip, anger, judgment, pride, and resentment in the community.

During the special service, several hundred men and women humbled themselves together before God. There were tears of repentance, followed by tears of joy, great rejoicing, and praise. That night God set many people free from their bondage to bitterness and unleashed His power on His church.

Some years ago, we had the joy of watching God send the fire of His presence to a Midwestern town of about eighteen thousand people. A lost businessman and his family were among those who were deeply impacted by that revival. Here's how Stu Duerstock recalls the events of those days:

A Banker's Testimony

In the fall of 1975, I was a thirty-eight-year-old bank vice-president with little spiritual interest. Our family belonged to a liberal church and was content with Sunday morning church attendance. (That was the socially acceptable thing to do.)

Then God visited our town in an extraordinary way, and my whole life was changed.

Two years earlier, the largest fundamental church in town had split in a vicious floor fight. Several hundred people had walked out and started a new church across town.

Although not a member of either church, I knew all too well how the resulting animosity and hostility had polarized the town. Families were split apart; friends who had known each other for years would cross over to the other side of the street to avoid speaking to each other; men who worked side by side at a large manufacturing plant in town had refused to talk to each other for the entire two years!

Needless to say, the testimony of Christ was not a good one as many like myself observed and thought, "What in the world is wrong with these people? Why can't they get along?"

However, when God came in revival, He melted the hearts of those two churches back together again.

One day, in the midst of the moving of God that was taking place, I turned on my car radio and heard the pastors of the two reconciled churches telling how God had broken down the barriers and replaced bitterness with love and forgiveness.

I found myself pulling my vehicle off the road and crying like a baby, under the convicting power of God. (I later found out that another businessman traveling through town was gripped by that same power. Although he knew nothing about the revival that was taking place, the power of God as he entered the city limits was so great that he, too, was compelled to pull off to the side of the road where he wept openly, confessed his sins, and got right with God.)

I drove immediately to the radio station to talk to the preachers and the Life Action staff, who by that time were conducting simultaneous revival services in both churches. I told them how I had been moved by the power of God as I listened to that radio program. They invited me to attend one of the meetings. I finally agreed to go when our neighbors extended another invitation. The first night my wife and I attended the services, I heard, perhaps for the first time in my life, the Word of God.

A couple of days later, God used one of the Life Action staff members to show me from the Word of God that I needed to be saved. At 3:15 on that Thursday afternoon, as we sat in a local restaurant, I bowed my head and trusted Jesus as my Savior. That day not only changed my eternal destiny, but the future direction of my entire family. As soon as I walked in the door of my home, my wife said, "There is something different about you." She was right. My heart was different, and my life and future were in God's hand for the first time in my thirty-eight years.

As God worked in my life, He continued to move dramatically in both churches. One night one of the pastors loaded his church members into a fleet of buses and journeyed across town to meet with the congregation of the other church. The two churches sought forgiveness from each other, many believers from both churches got their hearts right with God and with each other, and the glory of God descended on that service. No one who was present that night will ever forget how people wept openly, and how people who had not talked to each other for two years embraced each other and asked forgiveness for their bitterness and lack of love.

A picture was taken in that service which was placed in a full-page newspaper ad in which both churches publicly asked forgiveness from the entire community.

The impact of that revival has proven to be a lasting one in the lives of those who continued with God. Within two years, our family had surrendered for full-time Christian service. God confirmed that He wanted us out of the banking and insurance business, and working with people instead of dollars and cents.

I know that scores of other people have been saved, transformed, and revived as a result of what God did in those days of revival. I praise God that He was there, and that He did a mighty work! To Him be all the glory.

Do you long, as I do, to see the fire of God fall on your life, in your church, and in our nation? How badly do you want to see the glory of God descend? What price are you willing to pay to get it? Are you willing to sacrifice that which is most precious to you? Are you discontent to go on living without it? If so, join me in crying out to the God of Elijah, the God of fire:

Revive us again—
Fill each heart with Thy love;
May each soul be rekindled
With fire from above.

Hallelujah, Thine the glory!
Hallelujah, Amen!
Hallelujah, Thine the glory!
Revive us again.

Bring Back the Glory

Part Four

Chapter 11

When God Takes Over

Reflecting on a revival that God had sent to her life and her church two years earlier, one lady observed, "Revival is not just an emotional touch; it is a complete takeover!"

Genuine revival occurs when God takes over the church. Sinners become convicted of their sin, and people get right with God and with each other. Reality replaces hypocrisy, and truth casts out error. When God takes over, sin is renounced and self is surrendered. All self effort and human credit are obliterated by His presence. The church is ablaze with His glory and all else fades into insignificance.

In my twenty years of revival ministry, I have been privileged to witness many occasions on which God completely took over a life, family, or a church. In a few instances, the scope of God's blessing expanded to include an entire community. When God comes in the way I am talking about, He predominates above all else. People are so deeply moved by His presence and power that their lives are profoundly and lastingly changed.

In some instances, God has been pleased to take over the heart of an entire church. The first time I witnessed such a corporate moving of the Spirit was in Lynchburg, Virginia. Elsewhere, Dr. Jerry Falwell has told the story of what God did during those days:

Glory in The Church

Prior to October 11, 1973, I must confess that I had never witnessed a real revival.

Our church is known throughout the world for its ministry and evangelistic, soul-winning efforts. Yet, prior to the autumn of 1973, we had never experienced the power of revival. On the seventh of October, the Life Action Crusade team arrived at Thomas Road for a scheduled week-long evangelistic crusade—or so I thought.

At first the meeting began slowly, but not without significant blessings. On Sunday night, the seventh of October, Del preached on "Phony Baloney Christians." Over fifty people were saved that night, including many professing Christians. Our youth director, Rev. Vernon Brewer, immediately came under deep conviction about the assurance of his own salvation and gave a public testimony the following night of God's dealing in his life.

On Monday morning, during the chapel service for the Lynchburg Baptist College, one of Life Action's associate evangelists preached on "Ten Evidences of Salvation." Several more professing Christians were genuinely saved. Like the preaching of young Jonathan Edwards during the Great Awakening, these young preachers kept hammering at the evidence of change that ought to characterize genuinely reborn believers.

During the week, the meeting progressed with a quiet awesomeness. After Tuesday night's message preached on "Revival in the Family," over one hundred families publicly committed themselves to a regular time of family devotions. As a pastor, I was amazed and deeply concerned to discover how few fathers were actually leading their families in regular family devotions.

On Wednesday night, Del preached on "Having a Clear Conscience with God and Man." Attendance numbered 3,500 and the power of God was overwhelmingly evident in the service. However, during the invitation for people to clear their consciences with one another, something seemed to stall the earlier conviction. Perhaps the size of our auditorium made it difficult for people to find each other in the crowd.

The events of Thursday, however, convinced me that the size of a church is no deterrent when revival comes from God. God doesn't care whether He is working with just three or three thousand. From a human standpoint, I am sure we all left Wednesday night a little discouraged. Yet, the Holy Spirit's conviction was still heavy upon every heart.

During the school day on Thursday, there were no scheduled chapels. The Life Action team gathered off campus for a time of soul-searching, prayer, and fasting. Then, totally unknown to our church staff, something began to happen. The Spirit of God, almost mysteriously, began to overwhelm students in our academy. A high school student suddenly burst into tears and asked to be saved right in the classroom. A teenager from another class went to the principal asking him how to be saved. Soon, spontaneously and totally unrelated, dozens of students came under such intense conviction that many classes had to be turned into counseling rooms. Our principal, Vern Hammond, reported to me that "School has been called off in the favor of God!" Before the day was over nearly fifty young people had been gloriously saved.

The crowd came in Thursday night totally unaware of what had happened earlier. There was no sermon preached at all in that service. Prior to the scheduled message, the opportunity was given for people to share a brief testimony of what God was doing in their hearts. The response was tremendous. Dozens of young people and adults testified to God's working in their own lives and their families. After an hour of testimonies, an invitation was extended to those with whom God was dealing to go to the prayer room to meet alone with God. Ninety-nine people were saved that night!

Later that evening, the Life Action staff met with students in the lobby of our downtown dormitory for the nightly "rap session" and prayer meeting they had been conducting with our students. Over five hundred students crammed into the lobby. Kids were sitting on the stairways, table tops, everywhere. The "rap" time was set aside for a prayer meeting. The students joined hands and began to call on God for revival. Again a deep sense of conviction came over our college students. Only the record books of heaven know how many were saved that night. Several were still being counselled at 2:00 a.m. when the prayer meeting closed with the singing of "Jesus, There's Just Something About That Name."

Afterward, several individual prayer meetings continued throughout the night. Spontaneous singing and weeping could be heard all over the dorms. Yet there was not one incident of extreme behavior. By Friday morning, the entire church and campus were electrified. Classes went on as usual until the 10:00 chapel service. Again there were testimonies from the students, and again God moved. Students quietly left their seats and made their way to the prayer rooms. The chapel service lasted two and a half hours. For the second day, the school schedule had been interrupted in favor of revival.

I had never before seen anything like it. I had read about revivals of the past, but until that week I had never really seen one. Our staff met with the Life Action directors and the decision was made to continue the crusade. We were ready to cancel everything in favor of God.

On Friday evening, during the early part of the service, the Life Action Singers presented their multi-media high school assembly program on drugs and suicide. Another hundred, this time mostly adults, were converted that night. The prayer rooms were packed, tears were flowing, and everywhere people were smiling and praising God for what He was doing. People were reluctant to leave the service. They seemed to want to bathe in the atmosphere of God's Spirit.

More spontaneous prayer meetings were starting in homes and throughout the dorms. That night nearly one thousand students went to pray in the dormitories.

Several students, in light of Christ's imminent return, were deeply concerned for unsaved loved ones. Many called home long distance and led their parents to Christ over the phone. Some even drove home to urge their families to trust the Savior. One young seminary couple drove twelve hundred miles home to win the wife's father to Christ. Suddenly there was a burst of soul winning among our students such as we had never before experienced.

Students went everywhere throughout Lynchburg witnessing the gospel of Jesus Christ. During the weekend God continued working. My office was constantly filled with people wanting to be saved. On Sunday morning the church was aflame with the glory of God! During Sunday School, we dispensed with the lesson to allow adults to share their testimonies. Some were married students, some laborers, some professional people, some were converted church members, some had never been in church prior to that week.

Every testimony rang with a clear expression of God's grace. Again, God moved. Dozens of people were saved. So many were coming under conviction that our "timing" was totally thrown off for our television broadcast. We went on the air with tears in our eyes. God was unbelievably at work in His church! The sacred atmosphere of the morning carried over into the television broadcast. People later wrote from all over the country to ask what God was doing.

A few testimonies were given in the church service, and after delivering a brief message on revival, I invited those who were lost to come to the prayer rooms. They began coming from every direction. People of every age and rank in life were being touched by the Holy Spirit. The service went on for two hours. Up until then, 323 had been saved, and before that morning was over, 250 more had been born again!

The nightly services continued throughout a second week with people being saved every night. After thirteen continuous days of services, 683 had been saved, and nearly everyone was baptized. God had visited the Thomas Road Baptist Church, and truly, it was an experience of "glory in the church."[1]

Whenever I think of a divine takeover, my mind goes back to another, more recent visitation of God. This one took place at Birchman Baptist Church in Fort Worth, Texas, in 1988. From outward appearances, one could have wondered if this church really needed revival. The congregation was growing, the Word was being taught faithfully from the pulpit, and many outstanding programs were in place. Hundreds of seminary students worshiped regularly at Birchman. Over the years, this particular church had sent hundreds of its members out as full-time overseas missionaries—more than any other church in its denomination.

But God wanted to reveal His glory to these believers in a fresh, new way. Beginning in a crusade that continued for six weeks, God moved in and took over that church and would not let go. "Our team just happened to be the instrument God used at that time," observed Byron Paulus, the national administrator of our ministry.

The people prayed earnestly for several weeks prior to the crusade. Even before that, God prompted two men in the church to meet for prayer every Sunday morning at 6 a.m. to call upon God for revival. Brother Miles Seaborn had pastored that church for twenty-one years. His strong commitment to practical application of the Scripture had served to cultivate the ground and had prepared the people's hearts for revival. When God began to move, the pastor himself said, "God began to convict me that I was not dependent upon Him. I was so busy serving Him that I was neglecting Him."

Contrary to what we expected, the first few services of that crusade were unusually difficult as we sensed the intellectual pride of so many students and laypeople who were thoroughly familiar with the Scripture. But one night in the first week of the crusade, one of the gentlest, meekest women in the church asked if she could share something with the congregation. She confessed to spiritual pride and asked God and the church to forgive her. "I have taught your children in Sunday School," she acknowledged brokenly, "but I have taught them in the flesh. I haven't prayed over these children or these lessons like I ought."

Something about her testimony seemed to soften other hearts, and for the next six weeks, wave after wave of conviction, brokenness, and release moved throughout that congregation.

People confessed to cheating the government on their taxes and paid it all back. People confessed to stealing from the church by misappropriating small amounts of cash in the church's day-to-day business. College and seminary students confessed to cheating on their exams and made it right. Couples confessed infidelity to one another, the invisible barriers of guilty consciences were removed, and the spirit of many marriages was restored.

Night after night the prayer room was filled with people with broken hearts who emerged free, delivered from the bondage of every conceivable sin, ranging from bitterness and lukewarmness to bulimia, homosexuality, and occultic practices. It was a glorious sight to sit back and watch God at work deep within the soul of that congregation.

Let me share with you, in his words, some of Pastor Miles Seaborn's observations about what God did in his church during those weeks.

Birchman Revival

God touched down at Birchman Baptist Church, and we have experienced revival in a way never before known in the eighty-five year history of our church. Hundreds of individual lives have been changed, marriages have been restored or revitalized, immorality in all its forms has been confessed and repented of, "those who stole steal no more," and restitution of thousands of dollars has been made to former employers, the IRS, family members, businesses, banks, hospitals, etc.

Revival has come to salesmen, printers, store managers, preachers and church leaders, secretaries, schoolteachers, computer experts, nurses, dentists, doctors, veterinarians, bricklayers, housewives, CPA's, postal workers, electrical contractors, military personnel, beauty operators, counselors, students from grade school through graduate school, and on and on. These have been broken before the Lord, have confessed their sins, and are experiencing the continuing joy of forgiveness and an obedient life. They are reaching out in love to each other and to others in and out of the church.

Let me share a few examples of what God has done:

From a shop manager: "I was just thinking about the cost of what we have received free of charge. If we added up the hours and hours of family, marriage, financial, and personal spiritual counseling at $75 per hour, plus all the free printed material, magazines, etc., the amount would be phenomenal! I want to request that we keep the prayer room—I've gone to it dozens of times to get things right with God when He spoke to me. When the young man shared about quitting his job because of having to deliver pornographic literature, I thought, 'Well, at least that is one thing I haven't done!' Then God reminded me that when I worked at a printing company one time, we were low on business and took in one of those magazines. I had to work with the pictures and everything—so back to the prayer room I went!"

From a CPA as he stood with arms around his eldest son: "One Sunday morning, Tim St. Clair was preaching about bitterness. I listened to the sermon, but I really didn't think I was bitter toward anyone, because I thought I liked everybody. Tim asked us to pray and ask God to reveal to us if there was any bitterness in our hearts toward anyone. As I prayed, my oldest son's face flashed right in front of my eyes. I asked God, 'Am I really bitter toward my son? What has he done?' Then it came together and God helped me understand.

"You see, my son was born when I was seventeen years old. I went from being a teenager to being a father. During the past ͵ years, I had always been hard on him, but I thought, 'Well, that's just a father's way of making his son act the way that he should.' Then God revealed to me that I was bitter toward my son, and had blamed him for changing my life drastically when I was seventeen years old. I felt his birth interfered with our lives, and I took out my frustration on him, but it certainly wasn't his fault. Right then, during the service, I asked my son to go to the prayer room with me and I asked him to forgive me for being so bitter and hard on him all these years, because he just wanted to be a little boy and wanted his dad to love him."

From a businessman Sunday School teacher: "God dealt with me about my sins the first week, but it was not until the third week that I began to obey. My life was like the fake Rolex watch I wore—it looks good on the outside, but inside there is nothing of value." This young man went back to all of his family members, including an uncle from whom he had stolen, to former employers, and to his former commanding officer, to confess and make restitution for wrongs he had committed.

Just this week, he was rocking his baby and feeling good about a clear conscience when the Lord reminded him he had one more thing to clear up. He had lied on his application to General Dynamics, where he holds a five-security level job. In obedience he has gone back to his supervisor and confessed this sin, and the outcome is still pending as it goes to each of the five levels. He knew he might lose his job or even go to jail, but was willing to take that chance in order to be clear before God.

From the sister of an AIDS victim: "The revival found me dead inside. I had built my life around my brother whom I had placed before all others, including my husband and child. My generous husband paid huge telephone bills every month so I could talk to my brother every day, and my attitude for the day was determined by how he felt.

"My god died August 8 and I died with him, but I want you to know I have experienced revival and new life! I really repented when I ran down those stairs Wednesday night and talked and prayed with Brother Miles. I have asked forgiveness from my husband, my family, and everyone I know that I have offended, and I have made restitution as needed. I now realize that I serve a God who will never die, and I've found joy in God's Word and in being with God's people that I never knew before."

From a housewife: "When I heard about a two-week revival, I thought, 'Great, I'll work in the nursery all I can and make all the money I can.' But the first night I went, I asked to be relieved of my paid work so I could attend. The revival found me addicted to soap operas and a glutton! I have confessed these to God and have asked His forgiveness, and He has completely changed my life."

From a secretary: "At the beginning of 1988, my prayer for my family was that each of us would have a deep hunger and thirst for righteousness (Matt. 5:6). This was shared on a prayer card at the beginning of revival and God gloriously answered that prayer in my own and my husband's lives, our four children and their spouses. They shared how God has changed their lives. I had been praying six things for my church for eight years; God answered all six during the revival."

From the pastor: "God found me with disbelief that He could change me. He found me able to go through all the ministries of a large metropolitan church in the flesh. I know how to prepare sermons, how to witness, administer a staff, visit the sick and dying, and it found me going through the motions and saying, 'God, I'll tip my hat to you, but I can do this.' Few times did I ever come to God and say, 'This is beyond me.' I'd just work harder and more hours and visit and encourage more people.

"So revival found me working in the flesh in my ministry. It also found me having failed my precious family in a number of specific areas that had left them spiritually vulnerable. Once God broke in on my life, He began to deal with each member of my family, and then I saw person after person in our church stand broken before the Lord and our church family to tell what God had done in their lives."

Couple after couple have shared how God has restored their love for each other, of an openness in communication that they have never before experienced, of a oneness of spirit they have never known, and of a desire to share their lives with others. Pride and bitterness were uncovered again and again. Here are a few of the hundreds of written testimonies describing the way that God dealt with the sin of pride:

"God convicted me of pride in my life. Everybody thinks I'm a 'super Christian,' but I've really been spiritually dead for a long time. I try to get my friends to put Christ first in their lives without doing it myself. I want God to take complete control of my life and let Him have His way."

"God has found me empty, without power, frustrated by my own fleshly, unsuccessful efforts, defending myself, and trying to please others and save face. God said I was proud, self-centered, and in desperate need of His grace. I have fully agreed, confessed my sins, received His forgiveness, and left filled and empowered by His Spirit to allow Christ to live through me."

"God convicted me of having served Him with a prideful spirit, often cold, but always proud of serving."

"It has been years since I've expressed my need for Jesus. I've been struggling for a long time with why my spiritual life had no power, and my prayers were not answered. I've been playing a game, a phony. Jesus showed me tonight that it is me and my proud self that has been pushing me further from God. Tonight I yield myself to Him so that I will get out of the way, and He can live through me."

These are only the tip of the iceberg. The revival has continued though the Life Action Ministries team is gone. Every day brings new stories of God's marvelous grace and mercy! Praise Him with us!

THE AFTERGLOW

It had taken the Birchman Baptist Church nearly three years to raise $3.5 million to build a new 2,200-seat auditorium. Delays had kept them from moving in before the crusade began, so we met in the gymnasium. One night during the crusade, Pastor Seaborn shared with his people that he felt God had made them wait for revival so they would be ready to use that auditorium properly. "Lord, why can't we get into this building?" he kept asking. But God finally caused him to understand, "You want to fill that building with people, but first I want to fill the people with My *shekinah* glory!"

Shortly after the crusade ended, the congregation moved into that new building and every service was marked by the power of God's presence. "When we moved into that beautiful building," Pastor Seaborn said, "we were determined that we would never go back to being the church we had been. We have determined that this would be God's church. We kneel to pray, we weep, we share, and we confess. You can't let God take over like He did and then just go back to business as usual. This isn't even the same church any more."

Surely, times of testing will come in the days ahead. Satan is never pleased when God touches a church with His power. He will surely fight what is happening there, but I have observed that the deeper the revival, the longer its effect. People are still confessing sin, repenting, and getting right with God at that church today.

The glory comes when God takes over. He fills the church with His presence and power. When He takes over, all the credit goes to Him. Let it never be said that a man or a team brought revival to any church. Only God can send revival. Only He can ignite the flame of spiritual life and set the church ablaze with His glory.

Chapter 12

With All Your Heart

I will never forget the day I sat in the office of a world-renowned, silver-haired pastor and listened as he poured out his heavy heart. He reflected on earlier days in his ministry when he had witnessed the outpouring of God's Spirit in genuine revival. "But those days seem long gone," he confessed. "Oh, that God might do it again!"

The secret to those extraordinary movements of God was not in the methods, music, promotion, or preaching. There have been many revivals without great preaching, singing, or promotion, but there has never been a mighty revival without mighty praying.

Prayer is to revival what labor is to childbirth. The woman who expects to have a child must endure labor pains and travail prior to the joy of seeing that baby born. Likewise, there will be no revival apart from our willingness to agonize through the labor pains of prevailing prayer.

Prayer moves the hand of God to defeat the attacks of Satan against the kingdom of Christ. The reality of this truth moved Samuel Chadwick to write: "The one concern of the devil is to keep Christians from praying. He fears nothing from prayerless studies, prayerless work, and prayerless religion. He laughs at our toil, mocks at our wisdom, but trembles when we pray."

A church that is not a praying church may be large and widely-acclaimed; it may offer every conceivable type of program for every age group and interest; it may boast massive buildings, dazzling productions, and impressive statistics. But it will be a barren church, and it will never experience the manifest presence and glory of God in its midst. As R. A. Torrey expressed it, "The devil is not afraid of machinery; he is only afraid of God, and machinery without prayer is machinery without God."

UNLEASHING THE POWER OF PRAYER

Prayer unleashes the limitless, supernatural power of God into our circumstances. The marvelous promises of the Lord Jesus regarding the power of prayer stagger the imagination.

"If ye shall ask anything in My name, I will do it (John 14:14). "If two of you shall agree on earth as touching any thing that they shall ask, it shall be done for them of My Father which is in heaven" (Matt. 18:19).

"All things, whatsoever ye shall ask in prayer, believing, ye shall receive" (Matt. 21:22).

"Ask, and it shall be given you; seek, and ye shall find; knock, and it shall be opened unto you" (Matt. 7:7).

Throughout history, God's children have tested these promises and proven them to be true without exception. The pattern is generally the same: In the midst of dark and desperate days, God's people humble themselves and cry out to Him for deliverance. In accordance with His promises, God hears from heaven, extends mercy, and moves to meet the needs of His children; as a result, His name is glorified among the lost.

God's answers to prayer have punctuated twenty centuries of church history, and He is not about to stop now! Although earthly applause usually goes to the messengers of revival, heaven responds to those who pray for revival.

In the eighteenth century a little-known pastor in rural Epworth, England, knelt in his study and pled with God to send revival to his nation.

As he frequently requested his wife to keep their seventeen children from interrupting his prayer time, Samuel Wesley probably never imagined that the answer to his prayers was running up and down the hall outside that study. God raised up two of those children, John and Charles, to shake a continent for Christ.

Charles Grandison Finney stands as a giant in the records of revival in America. Only eternity will reveal how much of the spiritual fruit of his ministry was the result of the prayers of Brother Clery and Brother Nash. Day and night, isolated in dark, damp accommodations, these two prayer partners battled the forces of darkness as Charles Finney preached. In community after community, the fire of God fell in response to their earnest, prevailing prayer.

One of the great revivals in this century took place in Lewis, the largest island of the Outer Hebrides just off the coast of Scotland. Students of revival will associate the name of Duncan Campbell with that gracious visitation. Few, however, are familiar with Peggy and Christine Smith. Peggy was blind; her sister, Christine, was crippled with arthritis. Though little-known by men, they were well-known by God. Unable to leave their cottage even to attend church, these two godly elderly ladies sought God unceasingly until He opened the windows of heaven and poured out a mighty manifestation of His power that engulfed the entire island of Lewis.

With all my heart I believe God is able to turn the heart of this nation back to Himself. It is nothing for the omnipotent God of the universe to bring a hardened skeptic to repentance or to bring a backslidden church to her knees.

In light of the heart and power of God, the lack of intercessors in the church today is tragic beyond description. With a grieving heart, the ancient prophet cried out, "There is none that calleth upon Thy name; that stirreth up himself to take hold of Thee . . ." (Isa. 64:7).

Our generation has tried every conceivable way to experience spiritual reality. The need of the hour is not for better preaching, promotion, entertainment, programs, organization, seminars, conferences, television and radio broadcasts, techniques, or methods.

We are engaged in a battle "against principalities, against powers, against the rulers of the darkness of this world, against spiritual wickedness in high places" (Eph. 6:12). The battle cannot be won with weapons and strategies of men. The battle must be waged and won in the prayer closet with God.

Few subjects evoke a greater sense of guilt in the hearts of believers than prayer. We know that we ought to pray; we know that we need to pray; and yet, the vast majority of us don't pray. I think one of the reasons for our prayerlessness is that we don't realize the awesome potential of prayer. Our finite minds cannot begin to comprehend the power and the resources God has made available to His children. Faith-believing prayer is the means by which we lay hold of all that God wants to give us.

But we pray so little. So we whimper and whine when we ought to be filled with contentment and joy; we doubt and fear when we could be secure and confident; we strive and struggle in the energy of the flesh when we could be energized and empowered by His Spirit; we are overwhelmed when we could be overcomers; we live like spiritual paupers when, in fact, we are heirs of God with all His riches at our disposal; we trudge along in the ministry, bemoaning people's unresponsiveness when we could be witnessing an unprecedented outpouring of His Spirit. Why? "Ye have not, because ye ask not" (James 4:2).

Oh, if only we could visualize what God wants to do in and for and through us! If only we really believed that prayer is the key that unlocks all the vast treasure-stores of heaven and makes them ours!

SPIRITUAL WARFARE

Praying for revival involves entering into spiritual warfare. Until God opens our eyes, we can see only the physical realities around us. We forget that there is a great spiritual war going on behind the scenes. At this moment war is being waged in the heavenlies between the forces of heaven and hell. That fallen rebel, who once sought to establish himself as God, now moves ceaselessly throughout the earth and, aided by his loyal followers, seeks to maintain control over the minds and hearts of men.

God could choose to unilaterally disarm and defeat the evil one. But He has sovereignly ordained that He would move through prayer and fasting to loose the chains of darkness, to tear down satanic strongholds, and to release His supernatural power.

As we realize the great privilege of prayer as our number one weapon in the spiritual battles of life, we must be driven to our knees to pray. The Scripture promises: "The righteous cry, and the LORD heareth, and delivereth them out of all their troubles" (Ps. 34:17).

In the early church, when proclaiming Jesus as Messiah meant certain persecution, the harassed believers gathered together, not to lick their wounds or to plan a retreat, but to pray for boldness, before going back out to preach the gospel again (see Acts 4:29). Incarcerated in a Roman prison, Paul wrote to the church in Ephesus and asked them to pray "that I may open my mouth boldly, to make known the mystery of the gospel, For which I am an ambassador in bonds: that therein I may speak boldly, as I ought to speak" (Eph. 6:19,20).

The greatest investment we can make in the lives of those we love is to intercede for them in prayer. The greatest investment we can make in the life of the church is persistent, prevailing prayer on its behalf. What no amount of human effort, ingenuity, or preaching could ever accomplish, God can do, and He will do it in response to our prayers.

A PERSONAL APPEAL

I have recently been diagnosed with deadly cancer of the brain. While thousands of God's people are praying with me for complete recovery, I must face the fact that most of my earthly ministry may be over. Whether God chooses to restore me to health or to call me home, I would not exchange these last twenty years of ministry for anything the world has to offer. My highest aim and motivation have been to glorify

God through a surrendered life and through faithfully preaching the gospel and calling the church to revival.

With each passing year, my longing to see the glory of God in revival has intensified. It seems obvious to me that without a mighty moving of God's Spirit in our land, the future of America is grim indeed. Whether we are facing imminent collapse or the long-term consequences of our own decadence, our future will be a dismal one, apart from a divine visitation.

Like Old Testament Israel, we have forsaken the Lord and followed after other gods. The judgment of God against our sin has already begun to fall as He has begun to withdraw His presence from our society. In the absence of His presence, restraints against evil have been removed; unrighteousness is rampant.

Nowhere is the absence of God's presence more conspicuous or more lamentable than in the church. Nothing short of an outpouring of God's Spirit will revitalize and empower an impotent and anemic church to display once again His glory to a lost world.

I am convinced more than ever before that the only real hope for our churches and for our nation is an old-fashioned, Holy Spirit-empowered revival. No matter how unlikely the prospects of such a revival may appear at times, we must continue to exercise faith and to "seek the LORD, till He come and rain righteousness upon you" (Hos. 10:12).

I am often asked, "What will it take for revival to come to America?" I believe that it will take a complete willingness on the part of God's people to bow the knee to Christ as Lord and to His Word as the absolute authority for our lives. When we do, in His timing and good pleasure, He will send revival to His church and through us, immeasurable blessing to the world.

Of course, only God can send revival. You and I cannot manufacture it or make it happen. He alone is the Reviver. But you and I must meet the scriptural requirements of humility, prayer, seeking Him, and repentance (see 2 Chron. 7:14). We must allow God to break up the fallow ground of our hearts, to cleanse us thoroughly, and to fill us with the power of His Spirit.

The apostle Paul reminds us that God "is able to do exceeding abundantly above all that we ask or think." Then exercising faith in His power, Paul prayed that there would "be glory in the church . . . throughout all ages, world without end" (Eph. 3:20,21).

That is what revival is all about—glory in the church! When God's glory convicts, cleanses, fills, and empowers our churches, then the light of Christ radiating through us will penetrate the darkness of this lost world. When we stop pretending that things are all right and begin to cry out to God for mercy, then and only then can we expect a visitation from God.

There is a great cancer today in the body of Christ. While all may appear well on the outside, there is death and destruction on the inside. The gracious intervention of Christ, the wounded Healer, is our only hope.

When the prophet Malachi (4:5,6) closed the canon of Old Testament Scripture, he called for a prophet like Elijah who would come before the great and dreadful day of the Lord to turn the hearts of God's people back to Him before it was too late. We perhaps also stand on the precipice of a final era of God's grace to the church. And we, too, need prophets of God to call us back to Him before it is too late, that times of refreshing might come from the hand of God.

Revival, no matter how great or small in its ultimate scope, always begins with individual believers whose hearts are desperate for God, and who are willing to pay the price to meet with Him. Do not wait for God to use someone else. Let Him begin His refreshing, reviving work in you! Start to pray for God to stir the hearts of those around you. Ask God to direct you to two or three others with hungry hearts, and begin to pray with them.

I have been overwhelmed by the degree to which God's people have joined together in praying for me since learning of my condition. And I have been gripped with the thoughts of what could happen if we in the body of Christ would join our hearts with equal intensity to pray for an outpouring of His Spirit in genuine revival.

Thousands of believers from every possible background have come together to help bear my burden. They are motivated by a common concern, an impossible situation, and deep love. For the moment, they have put aside the differences that often divide them and have united their hearts to pray for a miracle in my body.

But is there not a far greater crisis in our churches today that cries out for the same attention? How I long to see such an intense, united prayer effort launched on behalf of the languishing, gravely ill church of Jesus Christ. What if we gave ourselves to the same kind of specific, sacrificial, persistent prayer that has been offered on my behalf? What if we were willing to pay the same price to believe God for a miracle of spiritual healing and revival in the body of Christ?

I believe that we would soon see the King in all His glory descend upon His church.

I could never adequately express what the prayers of God's people have meant to me in these days. I will always be deeply grateful for those who have sought God on my behalf. I do not know how God will choose to answer those prayers. I desire only His will, and if He will be most glorified through my homegoing, then I gladly embrace death and the joy that awaits me in His presence. But I know that nothing could bring greater joy to the heart of God than for a divine flame of His presence to sweep across this nation like a prairie fire, consuming everything in its wake, until His glory is revealed and this nation once again becomes a nation under God.

There are no human solutions that can remedy our spiritual condition, but there stands ready and waiting a Great Physician, risen with healing in His wings. And He will surely come to us when we seek Him with all our hearts.

Acknowledgments

On behalf of the author, who is now with the Lord, Life Action Ministries would like to express deep gratitude to the following individuals for their role in this work:

Del's wife, Mrs. Judy (Fehsenfeld) Parks, and his children, Del III, Danny, Joy, Jenny, and Jessica, for their willingness to sacrifice precious hours of their husband and father's final weeks on earth, so that he might deliver this message which burned so deeply in his heart;

Nancy Leigh DeMoss and Dr. Edward E. Hindson, for their work in compiling and editing this book from Del's recorded sermons, written articles, and taped interviews;

Sandra Hawkins, for her painstaking proofreading of the manuscript; Phyllis Janish and Rebecca Leachman, for their secretarial assistance; and

Gary McCauley, for believing and insisting that this message needed to be heard by the church.

About Life Action Ministries

Life Action Ministries is a family-centered revival ministry whose mission is to believe God for a genuine revival in the hearts of His people throughout North America, resulting in a spiritual awakening among the lost.

In one of his final messages before he entered the presence of the Lord, Del Fehsenfeld Jr. poured out the heart burden for revival that has always been at the crux of this ministry: "When a nation becomes as morally depraved, as spiritually blinded, and as steeped in humanism, hedonism, and materialism as America is, there is only one power in the entire universe that can meet and overcome such evil, and that is the power of the living God Himself, an outpouring of the Holy Spirit, a visitation of the manifest presence of God."

The vision God laid on Del's heart continues to burn in the lives of over 100 full-time staff members who are committed to carry the torch of revival.

The primary outreaches of Life Action Ministries include two-week revival crusades in local churches, multi-media musical productions ("America, You're Too Young to Die!", "The Family: Holding On for Life!", and "Bring Back the Glory"), camps and conferences, and revival publications (including *Spirit of Revival* magazine).

For more information about Life Action Ministries, or to schedule one of the Life Action teams in your area, or to begin receiving *Spirit of Revival* magazine, please contact:

Life Action Ministries
P. O. Box 31
Buchanan, MI 49107-0031
1/800/321-1538

Endnotes

Chapter 2

1. Charles Colson, *Against the Night* (Ann Arbor: Servant Publications, 1989), 19.
2. Douglas M. White, *Vance Havner: Journey from Jugtown* (Old Tappan: Fleming H. Revell, 1977).
3. Ibid.

Chapter 3

1. Charles G. Finney, *Prayer, The Keystone of Revival* (Minneapolis: Osterhus Publishing House).
2. Sammy Tippit, *The Prayer Factor* (Chicago: Moody Press, 1988), 125.

Chapter 5

1. Dony McGuire and Dottie Rambo, "When His Kingdom Comes" Copyright 1984, New Kingdom Music/ASCAP. All rights reserved. Used by permission of Benson Music Group, Inc.
2. Cf. John MacArthur, *The Gospel According to Jesus* (Grand Rapids: Zondervan, 1988) and his *Faith Works: The Gospel According to the Apostles*, 1993; Bailey Smith, *The Grace Escape* (Nashville: Broadman Press, 1991), Edward E. Hindson, *Glory in the Church* (Nashville: Thomas

Nelson, 1975). Contra, cf. Zane Hodges, *Absolutely Free!* (Grand Rapids: Zondervan, 1989) and Charles Ryrie, *So Great Salvation* (Wheaton: Victor Books, 1989). The great mistake of Hodges and Ryrie is reducing the gospel to mere assent apart from repentance and true faith.

Chapter 11

1. Excerpted from Edward E. Hindson's *Glory in the Church*, (Nashville: Thomas Nelson, 1975), Postscript: "The Story of the Lynchburg Revival," 118-126.